NAPOLEON AND HIS COURT

EQUESTRIAN GROUP OF NAPOLEON AND HIS STAFF AT AUSTERLITZ

(*From a print in Canon Brook-Jackson's collection, believed to be the only one in existence*)

NAPOLEON

AND HIS COURT

C. S. FORESTER

Simon Publications, Inc.

2003

Library of Congress Control Number: 25000910

ISBN: 1-931541-96-5

Printed by Lightning Source Inc. La Vergne, TN

Published by Simon Publications, P. O. Box 321, Safety
Harbor, FL 34695

CONTENTS

LIST OF ILLUSTRATIONS

NOTE.—*The illustrations are reproduced from prints in the collection of Canon Brook-Jackson, by kind permission.*

7

NAPOLEON AND HIS COURT

CHAPTER I

IN GENERAL

THERE was a time when France extended to the Baltic, the Ebro and the Tiber; when the term " Frenchmen " included Frenchmen, Spaniards, Italians, Belgians, Dutch, Germans and even a few stray Danes, Poles and Letts; when Rome was the second city of France, and Amsterdam the third; when the Emperor of the French was also King of Italy and Mediator of Switzerland; when one of his brothers was King of Spain, another, King of Westphalia, and one of his generals King of Naples; when all Germany was ruled by his vassals; when Poland was a French province in all but name; when Austria was the French Emperor's subservient ally; and when one of his less successful generals had just been appointed ruler of Sweden.

Never, since the days of the Roman Empire, had one man held so much power, and never in all history has so much power been as rapidly acquired or as rapidly lost. In ten years Napoleon rose from the obscurity of a disgraced artillery officer to the dignity of the most powerful ruler in the world; in ten more he was a despised fugitive flying for his life from his enemies.

9

It is difficult for us nowadays to visualize such a state of affairs. To the people of that time life must have appeared like a wild nightmare, as impossibly logical as a lunatic's dream. There seems to have been no doubt anywhere that the frantic hypertrophy could not last, and yet when the end was clearly at hand hardly a soul perceived its approach.

There was only one nation of Europe which escaped the mesmerism of the man in the grey coat, and that was the British. It was only in Britain that they did not speak of him with bated breath as " the Emperor," and remained undaunted by his monstrous power and ruthless energy. To the English he was not His Imperial and Royal Majesty, Napoleon, Emperor of the French, King of Italy, Protector of the Confederation of the Rhine, and Mediator of the Helvetian Republic. No, the English thought of him merely as Boney, a fantastic figment of the imagination of the other peoples of the world, who were of course a queer lot with unaccountable fears and superstitions.

But this Boney, this Corsican Ogre, incredible though he was, loomed appallingly large upon the horizon. There were beacons all round the coast in case he landed; his privateers were the scourge of shipping; prices were at famine point and business was parlous on account of his activities; the militia was embodied and there was a ceaseless drain of recruits into the army; every village mourned the loss of a son who had enlisted and whose life had been thrown away in some hare-brained expedition into ill-defined foreign parts. And yet on the other hand there were considerations which gave an aspect of unreality to the whole menace. England was constantly victorious at sea, and though Nelson might be mourned the glory of Trafalgar and the Nile cast the possibility of invasion into insignificance. The English people were confident that on land as well

they would beat the French at every encounter.
Not for nothing were Agincourt and Minden
blazoned on English history, and Alexandria and
Maida supplied whatever confirmation might be
desired. Such disasters as that at Buenos Ayres
were forgotten; confidence ran high. When
Wellington gained a victory by which all Portugal
was cleared of the French at one blow the public
annoyance that even greater results had not been
achieved, that the whole French army had not been
captured, was extreme. There were few English
people who did not think that, should Napoleon by
some freak of fortune land in England, the veterans
of Austerlitz and the almost legendary Imperial
Guard would be routed by the militia and the hasty
levies of the countryside. There was nothing which
could drive the realities of war hard home into the
public mind. If prices were high, then as compensation colonies fell into our hands, employment was
fairly good, and the business of manufacturing arms
and equipment was simply booming. Besides,
intercourse with the Continent was not entirely cut
off, for the smugglers worked busily and successfully, and French lace and French fashions and
French brandy circulated freely. It was hard for
the average Englishman to realize that the Corsican
Ogre was not merely an ogre, especially as the
fantastic cartoons of the period and the wild legends
which were current were more fitted to grace a
child's fairy-tale than to depict the most formidable
enemy England had yet encountered.

On the mainland of Europe the picture was
utterly reversed. The reality of war was only too
obvious. The Emperor was no mere cartoonist's
figure drawn with disgusting detail. They had seen
him; he had ridden into their capitals on his white
horse in the midst of the army which had shattered
their proud battalions over and over again. His

power was terrible and his vengeance was swift. In half the countries of Europe a chance word might result in the careless speaker being flung next day into an unknown dungeon. His armies swarmed everywhere, and wherever they went they left a trail of desolation behind them. The peasants were starved and the landowners were ruined, to pay the enormous taxes which the indemnities he imposed demanded. The mass of the people, who had once hailed the great conqueror because his arrival meant their delivery from feudalism, now found themselves crushed under a despotism ten times more exacting. The Emperor was very real to them. Many of them now served new rulers who had been imposed upon them by him, and him alone. Wherever he appeared he was attended by a train of subject kings to whom his wish was law. At his word an Italian might find himself a Frenchman, or an Austrian a Bavarian. And this was no mere distinction without a difference. Once upon a time the peasant classes cared little about the politics of their rulers, or even about which ruler they served. The fate of a professional army was a royal, not a national concern. But now every able-bodied man found himself in the ranks. Badeners fought Portuguese on the question as to whether a Frenchman should rule Spain, and a hundred thousand Germans perished in the northern snows because the Emperor of the French wished to exclude English goods from Russian ports. The imposition was monstrous, and in consequence the question of nationality became of supreme importance. If a country made war upon Napoleon every citizen of that country now realized that defeat meant the continuance of a slavery as exasperating as it was degrading. The fact that their eventual victory left them very little freer does not enter into this argument. It is sufficient to say that Napoleon was regarded on the

Continent with an interest agonizing in its intensity, and that this interest was nourished in a much more substantial fashion than prevailed in England.

It has been maintained and has infected all nationalities alike. The ability of the French nation to write telling memoirs is nowhere better displayed than in the period of the Empire. A large amount of very fascinating material was produced, by which the history of the period, which had previously been grossly distorted, was corrected and balanced. Details were worked out with an elaboration all too rare. The events in themselves were so exceedingly interesting, and the books about them were so well written, that it can hardly be considered surprising that more and more attention was turned towards the Empire. In addition, the fascinating personality of the Emperor concentrated and specialized the attention. More important than all, since events of huge importance turned merely upon his own whims and predilections, it was necessary to analyse and to examine the nature of the man who had this vast responsibility. It has become fashionable to inquire into every detail of his life, and there has grown up an enormous literature about him. Most of these books contain a fair amount of truth, but they nearly all contain a high proportion of lies. Napoleon himself was a good liar, but by now he is much more lied about than lying.

That coffee legend, for instance. Nine books on Napoleon out of ten say (with no more regard for physiology than for fact) that he was accustomed to drinking ten, twenty, even thirty cups of coffee a day. Napoleon drinking coffee is as familiar a figure to us as Sherlock Holmes injecting morphine, but both figures are equally apocryphal. The best authorities, people who really knew, are unanimous in saying that he never drank more than three cups a day. De Bausset, who was a Prefect of the

Palace, and in charge of such arrangements, distinctly says he took only two, and goes out of his way to deny the rumours to the contrary which were already circulating. This is but one example out of many; perhaps we shall meet with others later on.

It is necessary first to sketch Napoleon's career in brief, for the sake of later reference. The merest outline will suffice.

Napoleon began his military life under the old régime as an officer in the artillery; despite an inauspicious start, he attracted attention by his conduct at the siege of Toulon. Later he was nearly involved in the fall of Robespierre, but, extricating himself, he served with credit in the Riviera campaign of 1794. Next, he earned all the gratitude of which Barras was capable by crushing the revolt of the Sections against the Directory in 1795. By some means (it is certain that Josephine his wife had something to do with it) he obtained the command of the army of Italy; in 1796 and 1797 he crushed the Austrians and Piedmontese, conquered Piedmont and Lombardy, and made himself a name as the greatest living general. There followed the expedition to Egypt, where his successes (extolled as only he knew how) stood out in sharp contrast to the failures of the other French armies in Italy and Germany. Returning at the psychological moment, he seized the supreme power, and made himself First Consul. Masséna had already almost saved France by his victory at Zurich and his defence of Genoa, and Napoleon continued the work by a spectacular passage of the Alps and a perilously narrow victory at Marengo. Moreau settled the business by the battle of Hohenlinden. During the interval of peace which followed, Napoleon strengthened himself in every possible way. He codified the legal system, built up the Grand Army which later astonished the world, disposed of Moreau

GENERAL BONAPARTE

and various other possible rivals, assured the French
people of his political wholeheartedness by shooting
the Duc d'Enghien and by sending republicans
wholesale to Cayenne; and finally grasped as much
as possible of the shadow as well as the substance
of royalty by proclaiming himself Emperor and
receiving the Papal blessing at his coronation. But
already he was at war again with England, and the
following year (1805) Russia and Austria declared
against him. He hurled the Grand Army across
Europe with a sure aim. Mack surrendered at Ulm;
out of seventy thousand men only a few escaped.
At Austerlitz the Russian army was smitten into
fragments. Austria submitted, and Napoleon
triumphantly tore Tyrol and Venetia from her, gave
crowns to his vassal rulers of Bavaria and Würtemberg, and proclaimed himself overlord of Germany
as Protector of the Confederation of the Rhine.
His brother Louis he made King of Holland; his
brother Joseph King of Naples; his brother-in-law
Murat Grand Duke of Berg. Prussia demurred,
and was crushed almost out of existence at Jena.
Russia, tardily moving to her support, was, after a
hard fight at Eylau, beaten at Friedland (1807).
At Tilsit the Emperors of the French and of Russia
settled the fate of Continental Europe, and Jerome,
the youngest brother of Napoleon, was given a new
kingdom, Westphalia.

So far, nothing but glory and progress; but from
now on, nothing but false steps and failure. First,
the overrunning of Spain and the proclamation of
Joseph as King of Spain. This brought Napoleon
into contact with the enmity of a people instead of
that merely of a king. It gave England a chance of
effective military intervention, and it shook the
world's belief in the invulnerability of the Colossus
by the defeats of Vimiero and Baylen. Austria
made another effort for freedom in 1809, to submit

tamely, after one victory and two defeats, when the
game was by no means entirely lost. Hence
followed further annexations and maltreatment.
Then came blunder after blunder, while the Empire
sagged through its sheer dead weight. The divorce
of Josephine lost him the sympathy of the fervent
Catholics and of the sentimentalists. The marriage
with Marie Louise lost him the support of the
republicans and of Russia. He quarrelled with his
brother Louis, drove him from the country and
annexed Holland. He tried to direct the Spanish
war from Paris, with bad results. Annexation
followed annexation in his attempt to shut the coasts
to English trade. The Empire was gorged and sur-
feited, but Napoleon was inevitably forced to
further action. Having irritated each other past
bearing, he and Alexander of Russia drifted into
war, and the snows of Russia swallowed up what few
fragments of the old Grand Army had been spared
from the Spanish and Danube campaigns. It was
like a blow delivered by a dazed boxer—powerful, but ill-directed and easily avoided, so that
the striker overbalances by his own momentum.
Napoleon struggled once more to his feet. In 1813
he summoned to the eagles every Frenchman
capable of bearing arms. But one by one his friends
turned against him. Prussia, Austria, Saxony,
Bavaria, each in turn joined the ranks of his enemies.
His victories of Lützen, Bautzen and Dresden were
of no avail. At Leipzig his army was shattered; he
fought on desperately for a few more months, but
at last he had to submit and abdicate.

A further effort after his escape from Elba
ended with the disaster of Waterloo, and merely led
to the last tragedy of St. Helena.

So much for the general. From this we can turn
with relief to the particular; and from the particular,
with perhaps even more relief, to the merely trivial.

CHAPTER II

THE MAN HIMSELF

OF course, we all know him. He was rather short and corpulent, and he wore a cocked hat, a green coat with red facings, and white breeches. Sometimes, when the mood took him, he would appear in trailing robes, with a wreath of laurel round his forehead. Very appropriate, admittedly, but—that wreath does appear a little incongruous, does it not? Then there are times when we see him on a white horse in the midst of the battle. One or two dead men are lying near him in graceful attitudes; one or two others are engaged in dying still more gracefully. His staff is round him; in the distance are long lines of infantry and volumes of cannon-smoke. But everything is so orderly and respectable that one cannot help thinking that even in that discreet, dim distance the dying are as careful about their manner as was Cæsar at the foot of Pompey's statue. Verestchagin and others strike a different note, but they never saw Napoleon alive. We have portraits and pictures innumerable, but are we any nearer to the man himself—to what was inside the green coat and the cocked hat?

It is the same when we come to read the mountains of memoirs which have been written around him. There are solemn memoirs, there are indiscreet memoirs. There are abusive memoirs, there are

B · **17**

flattering memoirs.   There are memoirs, written in
all honesty, during the reading of which one cannot
help feeling that the writer would really like to begin
personal pronouns referring to Him with a capital
letter.   And yet, after months—years, perhaps—of
reading, one still feels that one knows nothing of
him.   One realizes, naturally, that he was a marvellously clever man, with a marvellous sense of his own
cleverness.   But of the man himself, of his little
intimate desires and feelings, one remains ignorant.
A century of memoir-reading will not do as much
for us as would, say, a week's sojourn alone with him
on a desert island.   What adds point to the argument is that obviously the writer of the most
intimate memoirs was just as far from him as we are.

The fact of the matter is that Napoleon in all his
life never had a friend.   From his adolescence to his
death there was nobody to whom he could speak
unguardedly.   It was not so much that he posed, as
that he had himself well in hand on all occasions.
He could unbend; he could pinch a grognard's ear
or crack jokes with his Guard; he could write passionate letters to Josephine or supplicatory ones to
Walewska; but we realize that each of these displays
is merely a flash from some new facet of the gem.
To the design of the whole, to the light which glowed
within secretly, we are perforce blind.

His tastes in art, which would be a valuable
indication to his character, are variously rated by
contemporaries.   One thing is certain, and that is
that art did not flourish under the Empire.   A
heavily censored press acts as a drag upon the wheel
of progress in this, as in all other matters, but one
cannot help thinking that this cessation of development is due as much to Napoleon's lack of interest
in the subject.   David's hard classicism and Isabey's
futilities are the best that the Empire can show
in painting, while in sculpture (save perhaps for

Houdon), in poetry, in romance, in criticism, not one names survives, with the slight exception of Madame de Staël. There is no French contemporary with Körner who could bear a moment's comparison; there is not even any single achievement, like Rouget de l'Isle's of the previous decade, to which France can point with pride. Napoleon's own favourite works in literature make a rather curious list; tragedy was the only kind of dramatic literature which he favoured, although tragedy is the weakest part of the French drama, and in tragedy he ranked Corneille far above all others; Ossian's poems, despite translation into French, had a great attraction for him, perhaps because the exalted wording appealed to him in his moments of fantastic planning; Goethe, the greatest living poet, held no fascination for him; but Rousseau did. Indeed Rousseau's influence is clearly visible in many of Napoleon's own writings. Beyond this, there is almost nothing modern which received the seal of his approval. The classics he read in translation, and solely for the sake of their matter. Music was not specially liked by him; he tolerated it because it roused in him the same sensations as did Ossian's verse—it was a drug, a stimulant to him, but not a staple necessary. In painting he showed no special taste; the honours he gave David clearly indicate that he held no theories of his own on the subject. This list of likes and dislikes is non-committal; it can tell us little about Napoleon himself; and we are once more brought to an abrupt halt in our endeavour to discover what manner of man he really was.

Yet we can approach the question indirectly. Napoleon had no friend; there was never a time when he was taken off his guard. His soldiers loved him— stay! It was not love, it was adoration. That is the key to the mystery. It was not the love of one man for another; it was the worship of a God. But just as no man can be a hero to his own valet, so can no general be a God to his immediate subordinates. The rank and file could think of Marengo, of Austerlitz, of Jena, but what of the Marshals? At Marengo, France was on the verge of a frightful disaster. The slightest touch would have turned the scale, and Napoleon, hemmed in against the Alps, must have surrendered. What of France then, with a triumphant army at her frontier and not another regiment at hand? In the Austerlitz campaign it was nearly the same. Before Jena, Napoleon fell into error after error. Not until the next day was he made aware that only half the Prussian army had fought against him, and that he had recklessly exposed a single corps to meet the attack of the other half at Auerstädt. That Davout fought and won was Napoleon's good fortune, not the result of his skill.

Looking back on fifteen years of unbroken success, the private soldiers might well believe Napoleon to be a God, but the Marshals were near enough to him to see the feet of clay. For them there was neither adoration nor love. He was their taskmaster, and a jealous one at that, lavish of reprimand and miserly of praise. He gave them wealth, titles, kingdoms even, but he never risked rivalry with himself by giving any one of them what they most desired—military power. The Peninsular War dragged on largely because he did not dare to entrust the supreme command of three hundred thousand men to a single general. With gold and glory even misers like Masséna became eventually satiated, and one by one they dropped away from his allegiance when the tide turned. It fell to Marmont, the only one of all the Marshals who owed everything to the Emperor, to surrender Paris to the Allies and complete his ruin. Not one of the twenty-six paladins accompanied their master to Elba or St. Helena; that was left to the junior officers such as Bertrand, Montholon and Gourgaud, who had been near enough to him to adore, but too far off to see faults. Yet even to these, life with their idol became at times unbearable, and more than one of them deserted before the end. In men Napoleon could not inspire the love that endures.

As regards women, it is an unpleasant task to venture a definite opinion. An aura of tradition has gradually developed around Josephine's memory, and she is frequently looked upon as a woman who sacrificed herself for her love, and allowed herself to be divorced to aid her husband. Yet her most indignant partisan would not deny that she had much to lose beside her husband. The position of Queen of Queens; unlimited jewels; an unstinted wardrobe (and she was passionately fond of clothes); the prospect of the loss of all this might well have moved a woman to more tears even than Josephine shed. And of her affection for her husband one may be permitted to have suspicions. Her circumstances before the marriage were at least doubtful, and afterwards—those nasty rumours about Hippolyte Charles and others seem to have some foundation in fact.

Of Marie Louise mere mention is enough. When we come to discuss her later life and her conduct with Neipperg we shall find clear proof that she did not love Napoleon. The other women who came into his life are pale shades compared even to these two. With none of them was he in love, and none of them loved him, or came to share his exile. Madame Walewska visited him for a few days at Elba, but that was merely to seek further favours for herself and her son. After Waterloo she married; all her predecessors had already done the same. Women did not love Napoleon. We may picture Napoleon, then, going through life friendless and quite alone. Never a moment's relaxation from the stiffness of his

mental attitude of superiority; never the light of
friendship in the eye of man or woman; every single
person in Europe was either his slave or his enemy.
To say the least, his was an isolated position.   And
yet, was he unhappy?   Bourrienne tells us that in
the early Revolution days Napoleon walked the
streets, gaunt and passionate, with a lustful eye for
rich carriages, ornate houses, and all the outward
emblems of power.   The phase ended as soon as
power was his, and he passed easily into the condition
of isolation which endured for the rest of his life.
He was the Man of Destiny, the sole creature of his
kind, and he was happy.   His isolation never troubled
him in the least.   If ever he referred to it, it was in
terms of satisfaction.   He was guilty on more than
one occasion of saying that he was above all law, and
it is well known that he believed in his " star "; he
believed that he was marked out by some inscrutable
higher power (the limitations of whose exact
nature he never defined) to achieve unbounded success
and to wield a permanently unlimited power.   It is
difficult to imagine such a condition.   The most
ordinary or most modest man has usually an undying
belief that his own ability transcends all others, and
that Providence regards him with a special interest,
but deeper still there is almost invariably a further
feeling (often ignored, but usually obvious at a crisis)
that this simply cannot be so.   Even if this further
feeling does not become apparent, a man's sense of
humour usually comes to his rescue and saves him
from the uttermost absurdity.   But Napoleon's
sense of humour was only feebly developed, and in
many directions was totally wanting.   On the other
hand, there were certainly many reasons for his
classification of himself as a different being from
ordinary men.   He never turned his hand to anything without achieving much greater success than
his contemporaries.   If a codification of law was

required, then Napoleon codified laws, without one half of the difficulty previously experienced. He won battles over every general whom the Continent pitted against him. If a province was to be conquered, or, conquered, had to be reorganized, then Napoleon was ready at a moment's notice to dictate the methods of procedure—and he was usually proved to be correct. For twelve years, from 1800 to 1812, Napoleon did not know what it was to fail in any matter under his own personal control, while during that period his successes were unprecedented. Besides, there were more convenient standards of comparison. He was able to work at a pace which wore out all his subordinates, and he was able to continue working long after they had been compelled to confess themselves beaten. In his capacity for mental labour he stood not merely unequalled, but unapproached. Even physically he was frequently able to display superiority; his staff over and over again were unable to endure fatigues which he bore unmoved. Lastly, he was usually able to bend to his will anyone with whom he came in contact. The unruly generals of the Army of Italy in 1796 gave way to him, when he was little more than a favoured upstart, with extraordinary mildness. He induced conscientious men like Lefebvre to agree to the most unscrupulous actions. Alexander of Russia, smarting under the defeats of Austerlitz and Friedland, was won over in the course of a few hours' interview, and became Napoleon's enthusiastic ally.

There certainly was a great deal in favour of the theory that Napoleon was a very remarkable man, but not even the greatest of men is justified in believing that he is different from other men in kind as well as in degree. The fact that Napoleon really did believe this is highly significant. It hints at something being wanting in his mental constitution, something similar to, but even more important than a sense of humour. His shameless duplicity in both his public and his private concerns points to the same end. His inability to gain the lasting friendship of any of those with whom he came in contact is another link in the chain of argument. His complete disbelief in the disinterestedness of the motives of any single human being completes it. Napoleon was one of the most brilliant thinkers the world has ever seen ; he was the most practical and strenuous in action ; he enjoyed for twenty years more good luck than anyone has ever deserved ; but he had a meanness of soul unsurpassed in recorded history. As a machine, he was wellnigh perfect (until he began to wear out) ; as a man he was deplorably wanting.

CHAPTER III

SOME PALADINS

I T was a common saying in the Napoleonic army that every man in the ranks carried a Marshal's bâton in his knapsack. This was correct in theory, but in actual practice it hardly proved true. Every one of the twenty-six Marshals of the First Empire had held important commands before the rank was instituted.

Grouchy, the last Marshal to be created, was second-in-command of the Bantry Bay expedition in 1796, when Napoleon was just making his name; Jourdan had commanded the Army of the North as far back as 1794.

But if the title of Marshal was no more than their bare due, Napoleon certainly gave his generals other honours in plenty. One of them, Murat, he made a King; another, Bernadotte, after receiving the title of Sovereign Prince of Ponte Corvo, later became King of Sweden and Norway. Berthier was Sovereign Prince of Neufchâtel. Three other Marshals were created Princes of the Empire; thirteen were created Dukes; six, Counts; and the only one remaining, Poniatowski, was a Prince of Poland already.

Besides titles, wealth without limit was showered upon them. Suchet received half a million francs with his bâton; Davout in 1811 enjoyed an income, all told, of two million francs a year along with the unofficial dictatorship of Poland and the command of a hundred and fifty thousand men. It was Napoleon's habit to bestow upon his generals huge estates in each country he conquered. Lefebvre received the domain of Johannisberg, on the Rhine, which had once belonged to the Emperor of Austria and later passed to the Metternich family, while Junot received a castle and estate of the unlucky King of Prussia. Nearly every man of mark was given five thousand acres or so in Poland, with the attached serfs. And Napoleon was the Apostle of the Revolution!

The one condition attached to the gifts was that the recipient must spend as much as possible in the capital. So Parisian shopkeepers grew fat and praised the Empire; the Paris mob battened on the crumbs which fell from the tables, and a feverish gaiety impressed the onlooker. Out in the subject countries was nothing but a grinding poverty, and in the countries recently conquered by France the tax-collectors strove to gather in enough to pay the indemnities, and even the rats starved because the Grand Army had passed that way.

It is when we come to examine the careers of the Marshals that we first meet evidence of one of the most curious and significant facts of Napoleon's life. Everybody to whom Napoleon showed great favour; everyone who received his confidence; everyone, in consequence, who had appeared at one time to be on the direct road to unbounded prosperity, met with a most tragic and unfortunate end. Not a few of the worst set-backs which Napoleon experienced were due to the defects of those whom he had trusted and aggrandized, and many of his favourites, apparently too weak morally to endure the intoxication of success, turned against him when fortune ceased to smile upon him. Their deaths were tragic, and their lives were nearly all dishonourable.

Of all the Marshals, Berthier was the foremost in seniority, in precedence, and in favour. In every campaign which Napoleon fought, from 1796 to 1814, he held the position of Chief of Staff. The history of his military career during this period needs no repetition—it is one with Napoleon's. Every conceivable honour was bestowed upon him. He was given the sovereignty of the principality of Neufchâtel and Valangin; in 1809 the additional title of Prince of Wagram; he was appointed a Senator, a Minister, Vice-Constable of France and a Grand Dignitary of the Empire; at Napoleon's hands he received a bride of royal descent, in the person of a Princess of Bavaria; in 1810 the supreme honour was his of representing Napoleon at the preliminary ceremony of the marriage with Marie Louise. It seemed that he was one with Napoleon, his faithful shadow and devoted servant. And yet when Napoleon abdicated and was sent to Elba, Berthier threw in his lot with the Bourbons, and swore allegiance to them. Napoleon's return and new accession to power during the Hundred Days, in consequence placed him in a terrible position. He was torn between his new allegiance and his old devotion to Napoleon. The strain proved too severe. He died at Bamberg, just before Waterloo, having flung himself from a high window in his despair.

The second senior of the Marshals was Joachim Murat. Murat was fortunate in two ways. He was able to handle large masses of cavalry with decision on a battlefield, and he married the sister of the Emperor. There was very little else to recommend him for distinction, but these two facts were sufficient to raise him to a throne. Napoleon appointed him to the command of the cavalry of the Grand Army. He made him a Prince and Grand Admiral of France. Next came a sovereignty—the Grand

Duchy of Berg and Cleves, and two years later Murat mounted the throne which Joseph Bonaparte had just vacated, and became King of the Two Sicilies. So far, it was a highly satisfactory career for a man who had begun as the assistant of his father, the inn and posting-house keeper of La Bastide. Murat determined to keep his throne, and during the dark days of 1814 he turned against Napoleon, and marched at the head of his Neapolitans against the French. But retribution was swift. He lost his throne next year in a premature attempt to unite Italy, and in the end he was shot by the indignant Neapolitan Bourbons after the miserable failure of an attempt on his part to recover his crown after the fashion set by Napoleon in his descent from Elba.

It is, perhaps, a pardonable digression to consider here what might have happened had Murat retained his throne. It is certain that he would have been as progressive as the Austrians and his own weak nature would have allowed. It is possible that the United Italy party would have looked towards his dynasty instead of to the House of Savoy. The growing Napoleonic tradition would have aided. Perhaps to-day we might behold in the south a King of Italy descended from a Gascon stable-boy, to balance in the north a King of Sweden descended from a Gascon lawyer's clerk.

But to return to our former theme. So far we have seen two of Napoleon's favourites meet with violent deaths. There are many more instances. Bessières was a nonentity distinguished by little except his devotion to the Empire. He attracted Napoleon's notice in 1796, and his doglike faithfulness was a sure recommendation. Bessières became the Commander of the Guard; later he was created Duke of Istria and was given immense riches. Napoleon honoured him with all the friendship of which he was capable; it seemed not unlikely that a

throne would be found for him.   But Bessières died
in agony after receiving a mortal wound at Lutzen.

Then there was Ney, the brave des braves.   His
personal courage was almost his only title to fame.
When Napoleon attained supreme power, Ney was
a divisional general of the Army of the Rhine.
Under the Empire he became Marshal, Duke of
Elchingen and Prince of the Moskowa.   It was Ney
who made Ulm possible by his victory at Elchingen;
it was he whose attack beat back the Russians at
Friedland; to him is due much of the credit for
Borodino, while his command of the rearguard
during the retreat from Moscow is beyond praise.
And yet he was many times in error.   At Jena and
during the Eylau campaign his impetuosity was
almost disastrous.   He made several grave mistakes
during Masséna's campaign in Spain, 1810-1811.
At Bautzen in 1813 he lost a great opportunity, and
he was beaten later at Dennewitz.   It was his
vigour and his dauntless courage which recommended
him to Napoleon, who made full use of these
qualities to stimulate the hero-worship of his young
troops.   Ney received wealth, high command and a
princely title at the Emperor's hands.   Then he
helped to force the Emperor to abdicate.   However, he was unstable; he betrayed his new king and
went over to Napoleon during the descent from
Elba.   Napoleon entrusted him with the task of
staving off the English during the Waterloo
campaign, and he failed lamentably.   He lost a
great opportunity at Quatre Bras through having
allowed his columns to lengthen out; he shilly-
shallied all the morning of the 16th of June; he
ruined the campaign by his furious countermand to
d'Erlon in the afternoon; and finally at Waterloo he
wasted the reserve cavalry by his unsupported attacks
on the English squares.   And the Bourbons shot
him as soon as possible after the second Restoration.

Lannes, " the Bayard of the French Army," whom Napoleon had called " le braves des braves " before he gave the title to Ney, met with as miserable a fate. He had begun life as a dyer's apprentice at Lectourne, but enlisted at the opening of the Revolutionary wars, and was a colonel on Napoleon's staff during the first campaign of Italy. His fearless acceptance of responsibility, and his magnificent dash and courage while in action were his great assets, and Napoleon favoured him more than any of the younger Marshals, except Murat. It was largely through him that Napoleon found it possible to employ the strategic weapon which he invented—the strategic advanced guard. Victories as widely divided as Marengo and Friedland were directly due to Lannes, and he was proportionately rewarded with a Marshalate, a Colonel-generalship, an enormous fortune and the title of Duke of Montebello. But he was mortally wounded at Aspern, and died of gangrene at Vienna.

There was one Marshal whom Napoleon especially favoured who did not meet with a violent death. Nevertheless his end was more terrible by far than was Bessières' or even Lannes'. This was Marmont, who in 1796 was a young captain twenty-two years of age, but who gained Napoleon's regard to such good effect that he was Inspector-General of Artillery at twenty-six, governor of Illyria and Duke of Ragusa at thirty-four, and Marshal in 1809, one year later. But he failed in Spain, Wellington beating him thoroughly at Salamanca. In 1814 he dealt the finishing blow to the tottering Empire by his surrender of Paris. He seemed fated to be unfortunate. Pampered by the Bourbons, he mishandled the army in Paris during Charles X.'s attempt at absolute power, and ruined both the dynasty and himself. He dragged out the remainder of his life in exile, hated and despised

PRINCE JOACHIM
(MURAT, KING OF THE TWO SICILIES)

alike by Bonapartists, Legitimists, Orleanists and Republicans.

So much for the Marshals Napoleon liked; his favour certainly appears to have been blighting. Now for those whom he disliked.

When Napoleon finally got rid of Moreau, the man who succeeded in general estimation to the vacant and undesirable position of unofficial leader of the unofficial opposition was Jean Baptiste Jules Bernadotte. This man was one of the most despicable and successful trimmers in history. In Moreau's Army of the Rhine he had attained the rank of general of division, but he was in no way a talented leader. Just before Napoleon's return from Egypt he had intrigued to attain the supreme power, but over-reached himself. In Napoleon's *coup d'état* of the 18th Brumaire he hunted with the hounds and ran with the hare with remarkable success, assuring the Directory on the one hand of his unfaltering support, and yet joining the group of generals who accompanied Napoleon, but characteristically not wearing uniform. In addition, he had a convenient shelter behind a woman's petticoats, for with subtle forethought he had married Joseph Bonaparte's sister-in-law, Désirée Clary. Désirée was a jilted sweetheart of Napoleon's, and what with her hatred of the great man, Joseph's support, and Napoleon's horror of a scandal in his family (combined with a sneaking affection for her) Bernadotte made himself fairly secure all round. But he still continued to intrigue against Napoleon. During the Consulate an extraordinary conspiracy was discovered centring at Rennes, Bernadotte's headquarters. Bernadotte himself was undoubtedly implicated, but he somehow wriggled free from suspicion. To the Republicans he posed as a Republican; the Bourbons were convinced that he was on their side; actually he was working for his own hand, while, thanks to Joseph, he obtained his Marshalate and the principality of Ponte Corvo from the Empire.

In action, various unsavourily suspicious incidents occurred in connection with him. In 1806 he took advantage of an ambiguous order to absent his corps both from Jena and Auerstädt; the results of his action might have been far-reaching. Later Benningsen and the Russian army escaped from the trap Napoleon had set for them by capturing vital orders which were on their way to the Prince of Ponte Corvo. At Wagram his corps was routed and broken up.

But when, in 1810, the Swedes were seeking a Crown Prince for their country, he was the man they selected. Apparently their choice should have been agreeable to Napoleon. Was Bernadotte not the brother-in-law of the King of Spain, a connection by marriage of the Emperor, Prince of Ponte Corvo and one of the senior Marshals? Moreover, while Governor of Hanover, he had had dealings with the Swedes and had ingratiated himself in their esteem. Napoleon was furious, but he could do nothing, and Bernadotte became Crown Prince and virtual autocrat of Sweden. It only remained for him to win the favour of Russia by turning against France, so that, at the Treaty of Abo, Norway as well was handed over to his tender mercies.

Later he even angled for the throne of France, but the French could never forgive the part he had played in defeating them at Gross Beeren, Dennewitz and Leipzig; they did not realize that with this very object in view he had almost betrayed his new allies, and had hung back and procrastinated in order to retain his French popularity.

But double-dealer, intriguer, traitor that he was, hated by Napoleon, hated by the French people, despised by the rest of Europe, he nevertheless held on to his throne, and transmitted it to his descendants. Nowadays the House of Bernadotte is not considered too ignoble to wed even with a branch of the House of Windsor.

There were other Marshals whom Napoleon disliked, mainly because of their former association with Moreau. Macdonald was the son of a supporter of the Young Pretender, and was a relative of Flora Macdonald. He failed to pass the examination for a commission under the old régime, but with the Revolution came his chance. He distinguished himself under Dumouriez and Pichegru (who subsequently turned Royalist), and then under Moreau. It was an unlucky start for him. The Directory appointed him to the command of the Army of Naples, but with this force he was beaten by Suvaroff in the four days' battle of the Trebbia. Subsequently he performed the marvellous feat of leading an army across the Splugen in midwinter, but for all that Napoleon employed him as little as possible, keeping him on half pay until 1809. However, Macdonald received his bâton after Wagram; mainly, it is believed, to throw a stronger light on Bernadotte's failure. In 1813 Macdonald, Duke of Tarentum, was beaten again at the Katzbach, but by now Napoleon had some idea of his worth and retained him in command. By a delicious piece of irony, Macdonald the distrusted was the last Marshal to leave the Emperor in 1814; he was also one of the few to adhere to the Bourbons during the Hundred Days. He enjoyed great honour under the Restoration and the July Monarchy, and died comfortably in his bed at the age of seventy-five.

Another *bête noire* of Napoleon's was St. Cyr. He too was one of the "Spartans of the Rhine." In consequence Napoleon kept him out of active service as much as possible. This course of action was of doubtful utility, for St. Cyr was a man of superior talents. Not until 1812 was he made a Marshal, but wounds then kept him out of action until August, 1813, and he was made prisoner by the Allies in the autumn. The Bourbons, however, took kindly to him, and he held various high offices until his death in 1830.

Thus the five favourite Marshals of Napoleon died miserably, and the three whom he disliked would be said to have lived happily ever after by any self-respecting moral story-teller. It is a very curious fact, and one which finds a parallel elsewhere in Napoleon's career, as we shall see in later chapters.

CHAPTER IV

ONE WIFE

WE have already alluded to the intensely
needy period of Napoleon's life, which
was mainly centred around the year
1795. He knew himself to be a world conquerer;
he despised the shifty intriguers who controlled at
that time both his own destiny and that of France;
he bitterly envied the few insolent survivors of the
old noblesse whom he had met, while his very bread
was precariously earned. It was a maddening
situation.

Then circumstances suddenly took a change for
the better. By a happy accident Barras employed
him to put down the revolt of the sections, and
within a few days Napoleon found himself general
of the army of the interior, and a person of some
consequence. Still, there were bitter drops even in
this first draught of success, for his position depended
solely on the whim of the readily corruptible
Director, who could with a word have sent him
either to a dungeon or to a command-in-chief.
Moreover, the haughty Parisian society regarded
the gaunt, desperately earnest general of twenty-six
with an amusement they made no attempt to
conceal. Parisian society had had nearly two years
by now in which to concentrate, and it was already
crystallizing out. There were old sansculottes, now
Ambassadors, Ministers or Directors. There were

Army contractors in hordes. There were their wives (either by courtesy or by Republican law) who were just recovering from the *sans chemise* phase and beginning to ape the old customs of the *haut noblesse*. Finally there were a few of the old court families along with innumerable pretenders, ex-valets masquerading as ci-devant marquises; comtesses (as *précieuses* as they could manage) who had once been kitchenmaids, while every name hinted at a " de " which had been perforce dropped during the Terror. And because trifling was for the moment the fashion, this select band could well afford to sneer at the ridiculous little Corsican officer who meant everything he said, and who had had great difficulty before the Revolution in proving the three generations of noble descent necessary to obtain nomination as a military cadet.

Napoleon in these circumstances acted very much as he did in a military difficulty. He selected the most advantageous objective, flung himself upon it, and followed up his initial success without hesitation. He broke into the charmed circle of Directory society by marrying one of its shining lights.

Josephine, vicomtesse de Beauharnais, was a representative of the farthest outside fringe of Court society under the old régime. Her marriage with Beauharnais had been arranged by her aunt, who was her father-in-law's mistress. This unfortunate relationship, combined with poverty and the obscurity of the family, had barred most of the doors of pre-Revolutionary society to her, and the Beauharnais were, in the minds of the Montmorencys and Rohans, no more worthy of notice than the merest bourgeois. Of this fact Bonaparte cannot have been ignorant, no matter what has been said to the contrary, but it was of no importance to him. He cared little even for the fact that Beauharnais had

been at one time a President of the Constituent
Assembly and Commander-in-Chief of the Army
of the Rhine, before meeting the fate of most of the
Commanders-in-Chief of 1794. All that mattered
to Bonaparte was that Josephine was a member of
the narrow circle of the Directory, that in fact she
and Madame Tallien were the two most important
women therein, and that marriage with her would
gain him admission also. The Directory was fast
becoming a close oligarchy keeping a jealous eye
watching for intruders, and Napoleon had to act at
once. His policy was soon justified, for immediately
after his marriage his position was recognized by the
offer of the longed-for command of the Army of
Italy.

There were other considerations as well. Josephine possessed a wonderful charm of manner, and
her taste was irreproachable. The beauty of her
figure was undoubted; that of her face was enhanced
by dexterous art. To Napoleon, starved of the good
things of life, and incredibly lustful after them, she
must have appeared a houri of his Paradise. The
violence of his reaction from a forced self-control may
be judged by the stream of passionate letters which
he sent her every few hours during the opening of
his campaign of Italy. Heaven knows he had difficulties enough to contend with there, what with
mutinous generals, starving soldiers, and an enemy
twice his strength, but we find him snatching a few
minutes two or three times a day to turn from his
labours and worries in order to contemplate the joys
he had attained, and endeavouring to express them
on paper.

Josephine's motives were also mixed. She was
thirty-two years of age, and she was desperately poor.
Her late husband's property was almost entirely
situated in the West Indies, and it was now held by
the English. Her dreadful experiences under the

Terror, when she was imprisoned and within an ace of being guillotined, had probably aged her and shaken her nerve. Barras and various bankers had helped her with funds (perhaps expecting a return, perhaps not) but such resources would soon come to an end. In this extremity, appeared Napoleon, pressing an urgent suit. After all, he was not too bad a match. He was already general of the army of the interior, and between them both they ought to screw some better appointment out of Barras. He had not a sou to bless himself with beside his pay, but Republican generals usually found means to become rich in a short time. If he were killed, there would be a pension; if he survived, and was unsuccessful, divorce was easy under Republican law. She obviously stood to gain much and to lose little.

And then it could not be denied that Napoleon had a way with him. His fierce Southern nature would sometimes raise a response in her. After all, she was a Creole, and her Creole blood could hardly fail to stir at his passionate wooing. Although six years his senior, disillusioned, experienced, hardened and shallow though she was, there were times when his tempestuous advances carried her away.

Yet at other times, when he was absent, and she had once more caught the infection of cynicism and trifling from her associates, Napoleon appeared vaguely absurd to her. " Il m'ennuie," she would say, languidly turning the pages of his letters. She had no desire to leave Paris, where she was enjoying the prestige of being the wife of a successful general, to share with him the privations of active service. Only when Lombardy was in his hands, and a palace and an almost royal reception were awaiting her, did she join him.

Moreover, until she had a position to lose, she undoubtedly indulged in flirtations. Corsican

jealousy may have played a part in the furious rages
to which Napoleon gave rein, but there is no denying
that Josephine was several times indiscreet. In
turn, he suspected Hippolyte Charles, a young
and handsome army contractor, Murat (at that
time his aide-de-camp) and even Junot, his blind
admirer.

By the time that Napoleon was nearing supreme
power, his brief passion for Josephine had burnt
itself out. He himself had already been several
times unfaithful to her, and the only feeling that
still remained was the half-pitying affection a man
bears towards a discarded mistress. On his return
from Egypt he found elaborate preparations made
for him. His family, poisonously jealous of
Josephine, were waiting with circumstantial accounts
of her actions, and they pressed him to obtain a
divorce. Josephine, who had set out to meet him,
in order to get in the first word, had taken the wrong
road and missed him, so that the Bonaparte family
had a clear field. They made the most of it.
Josephine returned to Paris to find her husband
almost determined upon divorce.

At one and the same time Napoleon had to
endure the anxieties of the *coup d'état*, the urging
of his brothers and sisters and the appeals of his wife
and step-children. It must have been a severe trial,
and in the end he gave way to Josephine. Probably
he realized that it was the wisest thing he could do.
He could ill afford a scandal at this crisis in his career,
and Josephine was a really useful helpmate to him.
He paid off her debts (to the amount of a mere
hundred thousand pounds) and settled down to make
the best of things.

The lesson was not lost on Josephine. She was
now the first lady of the Continent, and never again
did she risk the loss of that position. Thenceforward
she lived a life of rigid correctness, and instead it was

Napoleon who became more and more unfaithful to her.

It was a strange period through which Josephine now lived. On the one hand she had reached heights of which she could never have dreamed before; on the other was the bitter probability that all her power and position would vanish in a moment when Napoleon made up his mind to take the plunge. The other Bonapartes were most bitterly hostile to her, and lost no opportunity of displaying their hostility. The only possible method of making her position permanent was to have a child, and this boon was denied her. And yet Napoleon found her a most invaluable ally. Her queenly carriage and perfect taste in clothes were grateful in a Court the awkwardness of whose manners was the jest of Europe. The majority of Frenchmen were honestly fond of her, and her tactful distribution of the charitable funds placed at her disposal by Napoleon enhanced this sentiment. In her meetings with royalty she was superb; she displayed the arrogance neither of an upstart nor of an Empress; the Kings of Würtemberg and of Bavaria grew exceedingly fond of her. Most important of all, perhaps, was the help which she gave Napoleon during the Bayonne Conference. The haughty grandees of Spain, the harebrained Prince of the Asturias and even the imbecile King himself showed her the deepest respect, despite the fact that Napoleon was endeavouring to coerce them into handing over the crown to his brother.

The occasions were rare, however, when Josephine was allowed to enter into more than the mere ceremonies of international politics. She was neither allowed to act nor to advise. At the least hint of interference on her part Napoleon was up in arms on the instant. Current rumour credited her with attempting to save the life of the Duc d'Enghien, and this has frequently been affirmed since, but from what we know of Napoleon and from what we know of Josephine we can only conclude that her attempt was timid and that Napoleon's refusal was blank and brief. For Josephine there only remained a purely decorative function. Other activities were denied to her (one cannot help thinking that she did not strive for them with much vigour); she was placidly content to spend her days in inspections of her wardrobe, in changing her toilettes half a dozen times daily and talking scandal with her ladies-in-waiting.

These amusements were not quite as harmless as might be imagined, for her passion for dress caused her to run heavily into debt, and every jeweller in Paris knew that he had only to send her jewellery for inspection for it to be instantly bought. To pay her debts she was put to curious expedients. She was in continual terror lest her husband should discover them, and she gladly paid enormous blackmail to her creditors to postpone the day of claim. She even appealed for assistance to Ministers and other high officials sooner than tell Napoleon. Naturally the storms which occurred when the day of reckoning could no longer be put off were terrible. Napoleon raged ferociously at every discovery. He paid the debts, it is true, but he usually arbitrarily reduced the totals by a quarter or even a half before doing so. Even then the tradespeople made a large profit, for they not only made allowance for his action, but they also took full advantage of Josephine's uninquiring nature.

The unstable situation dragged along, to the surprise of many people, to the consternation of many others, and to the delight of even more, for several nerve-racking years. The end had to come sooner or later, and it came surprisingly late.

CHAPTER V

THE DIVORCE

A T the close of 1809 Napoleon was at the height of his power. Every country of Europe, except England, was his vassal or his ally, and he was about to send Masséna and a sufficient force to Spain to ensure that England also would cease from troubling. The circumstances which were to lead to the fall of his enormous empire were already well developed, but they were hardly obvious to the common eye, which was dazzled by his brilliance.

The one element of weakness apparent was the lack of an heir to the throne. The equilibrium of Europe was poised upon the life of one man, and although many people believed that man to be super-human, there was no one who thought him immortal. Napoleon had been wounded at Ratisbon; perhaps at his next battle the bullet would be better aimed. But hit or miss, there were many would-be assassins in Europe, and knives were being sharpened and infernal machines prepared in scores of dingy garrets.

No one could imagine what would happen were Napoleon to die. The Marshals recalled longingly the break-up of the Macedonian Empire, and already in fancy saw themselves kings. The Republicans saw in his death the downfall of autocracy; the Royalists hoped for the restoration of Legitimacy. Subject nations saw themselves free; hostile nations saw themselves enriched. The one thing which obviously could not happen was the succession of the legal heir; Joseph in Spain, Louis in Holland and Jerome in Westphalia were at that very moment showing how unfit they were to govern anything. The Viceroy of Italy (Eugène de Beauharnais, Napoleon's stepson) was popular and capable, but Napoleon realized that on account of his lack of Bonaparte blood he would not be tolerated. There was one child who might perhaps have been accepted, and that was Napoleon Charles, son of Louis Bonaparte and Hortense Beauharnais. Vulgar gossip gave Napoleon himself the credit for being the father of his stepdaughter's child, and on this account Napoleon Charles was considered the likely heir, but he died of croup. It is possible that calamities without number would have been prevented had there been in 1807 an efficient nurse at the sick-bed of a child.

However that may be, Napoleon had no heir, and he had given up hope of Josephine presenting him with one. At the same time, any doubts he had on his own account were effaced by the birth of a son to him by Madame Walewska. He dismissed as impractical a suggested scheme of simulated pregnancy on Josephine's part; too many people would have to be in the secret; if they lived they would hold as much power as the Emperor himself; and if (as he was quite capable of doing) he executed everyone concerned, in Oriental fashion, tongues would wag harder than ever. Besides, although the French would apparently put up indefinitely with his losing a hundred thousand of their young men's lives a year, they would not tolerate for one second being made fools of in the eyes of the whole world.

Then Napoleon might have adopted one of his own illegitimate sons. Even this wild project he considered carefully, but he put it aside. The only course left open was to divorce Josephine and take some more fruitful wife instead, and Napoleon gradually came to accept this project.

Whether he was wise or not in this course of action cannot be decided definitely. Certainly he was not justified in the event, and he later alluded to the Austrian marriage as an "abyss covered with flowers." What he left out of full consideration when making his decision was that, while Europe might suffer his tyranny uncomplainingly if they believed that the system would end with his death, they would endeavour to end it at once if there were a chance of its continuing indefinitely. In a similar manner the birth of an heir to James II. of England had precipitated matters a century before. But whether Napoleon forgot this point, or whether he believed his Empire more stable than it actually was, he nevertheless determined on divorce and a new marriage.

On his return from the Wagram campaign of 1809, Josephine found him fixed in his decision. The connection between their apartments was walled up, and for weeks the Emperor and the Empress never met without a third person being present. It seems strange that the man who did not falter at Eylau, who sent the Guard to destruction at Waterloo, should have been daunted by the prospect of a woman's tears, but Napoleon undoubtedly put off the unpleasant interview as long as possible. At last he nerved himself to the inevitable, and the dreaded sentence was pronounced. An official of the palace tells a story of Napoleon's sudden appearance among the Imperial ladies-in-waiting carrying the fainting Empress in his arms. Ten days later, on the 15th of December, Josephine announced her acquiescence in the decision to the Imperial council, and the marriage was annulled by *senatus consultum*.

Napoleon had endeavoured to procure a more satisfactory form of divorce from the Pope, but Pius, to his credit, would not assist him. Five years before, at the coronation, he had refused his blessing until the Imperial pair had been married by the Church (the marriage in 1796 was purely a legal contract), and Napoleon, exasperated but compelled to yield, had submitted to a ceremony conducted by the Archbishop of Paris under conditions of the utmost secrecy. Pius could not in decency give his aid to break a marriage celebrated at his especial request only five years before, and in consequence he found himself a prisoner in French hands, and the last of the patrimony of St. Peter was annexed to the French Empire.

It would puzzle a cleverer man even than Napoleon to devise a series of actions better calculated to annoy the Church and its more devout followers.

For Josephine the pill was gilded in a style more elaborate even than was customary under the Empire. She retained her Imperial titles; she received the Elysée at Paris, Malmaison, and the palace of Navarre. An income of a hundred and fifty thousand pounds sterling per annum was settled upon her. No restraint in reason was set upon her actions; she was not forced into retirement; and Napoleon continued to visit her even after his marriage to Marie Louise. For the last four years of her life Josephine occupied a position unique in history.

Josephine bore her troubles well in public. However much she may have wept to Napoleon, however much she may have knelt at his feet imploring him to have mercy, to the world at large she showed dry eyes and an immobile expression. Perhaps her pride came to her help; perhaps, after all, freedom, the title of Empress, and a monstrous income, may have reconciled her to her loss of precedence; it is even conceivable that she preferred the sympathy of Europe, expressed in no uncertain voice, to the burdens of royalty.

Josephine all her life was a *poseuse* of minor mental capacity; what could be more gratifying to her than a situation where the possibilities of posing were quite unlimited?

For her, these possibilities were never cut short. She never had to endure the anticlimax of being the divorced wife of a fallen Emperor; she died suddenly just before Napoleon's first abdication, soon after receiving visits from all sorts of Emperors and Kings who were accompanying their armies in the campaign of 1814.

CHAPTER VI

ANOTHER WIFE

THUS at the beginning of 1810 Napoleon found himself once more unmarried, and free to choose himself a new bride. There never was a choice so fraught with possibilities of disaster. It was not so much a matter of making the most advantageous selection, as of making the least dangerous. If he married a woman of inferior rank, all Europe would exultantly proclaim that it was because no royal family would admit him. If he married a princess of one of his subject kingdoms, Bavaria, Würtemberg or Saxony, the others would become instantly jealous. A Bourbon bride was obviously out of the question, seeing that he was keeping all three royal branches out of their patrimonies. Should he choose a Hohenzollern, then the countries which held territories which had once been Prussian would become justifiably uneasy. There only remained the Hapsburgs and the Romanoffs, and a marriage with either would annoy the other. The best thing Napoleon could do was to ally himself with the more powerful, which was undoubtedly the royal house of Russia.

But here Napoleon met with an unexpected reverse. The Czar Alexander was at once a realist and an idealist, and he could not decide anything without months of cogitation. Moreover, the clever

advisers round him foresaw that Napoleon's demands
of their country must increase unbearably, and they
had no intention of tying their ruler's hands in this
fashion.   Torn between his ministers' advice and the
urging of his old admiration for Napoleon, between
his pride of race and his desire for a powerful alliance,
Alexander temporized and then temporized again.
He explained that all the Grand Duchesses were
members of the Greek Church, and he had qualms
about the necessary change of religion.   He tried to
show that they were all already affianced.   He said,
literally, that his mother would not allow him to act.

In the end, Napoleon, fearing a rebuff, and
conscious that delay would weaken his position,
abandoned the project and turned his attention to
Austria.   Alexander was naturally annoyed.   1812
may be said to have begun in 1810.

However, if a Grand Duchess were unavailable,
an Archduchess would certainly bring Napoleon
compensations.   The House of Hapsburg-Lorraine
was the most celebrated in Europe; it had supplied
Holy Roman Emperors since the thirteenth century.
After Napoleon and Alexander, Francis was easily
the most powerful continental ruler, despite his
recent defeats; Aspern and Wagram had just shown
how delicately the balance was poised.   But more
than this; the Hapsburgs and the Bourbons had
repeatedly intermarried; if there were anything that
would convince the doubters that Napoleon was a
real, permanent monarch, it would be his marriage
with the niece of Louis XVI, the daughter of His
Imperial, Royal and Apostolic Majesty the Emperor
of Austria, King of Hungary, King of Bohemia,
Duke of Styria, of Carinthia and of Carniola,
erstwhile Emperor of the Holy Roman Empire, and
titular King of Jerusalem.

The achievement would be deficient in some
respects.   Tyrol and Dalmatia no longer figured

MARIE LOUISE
EMPRESS OF THE FRENCH

in the Emperor's resounding list of titles—France ruled one and Bavaria the other, and Austria might easily demand restitution as the price of Marie Louise's hand. The very name of the new Empress would remind people of Marie Antoinette, her ill-fated aunt, and a family alliance between Napoleon and the autocrat of autocrats might well give the *coup de grâce* to the moribund belief in Napoleon as the Apostle of the Revolution.

Be that as it may, Napoleon had already gone too far to draw back, and early in 1810 he prevailed on Francis I. to make a formal offer of his daughter's hand.

They were an oddly contrasting couple. He was forty, she was eighteen. He was an Italian-Corsican-French hybrid of unknown ancestry, she was of the bluest blood in Christendom. He was the victorious leader of the new idea, she was the scion of a dying autocracy. Three times had Marie Louise fled with her family from the wrath of the French; all her life she had heard the man who was about to become her husband alluded to as the embodiment of evil, as the Corsican Ogre, as the Beast of the Apocalypse. They had never met, and she had certainly not the least idea as to what kind of a man he was. All things considered, it was as well that she had been trained all her life to accept her parents' decision on her marriage without demur.

Her training had been what might have been expected of the etiquette-ridden, hidebound, conservative, dogmatic House of Hapsburg. She was familiar with every language of Europe, because it could not be foreseen whom she would eventually marry. Music, drawing, embroidery, all those accomplishments which permitted of surveillance and which did not encourage thought were hers. But she was proudest of the fact that she could move her ears without moving her face.

D

Every possible precaution that she would retain her valuable innocence had been taken. She had never been to a theatrical performance. She had never been allowed to own a male animal of any species; her principal pets were hen canaries. Her reading matter was closely scrutinized beforehand, and every single word which might possibly hint at difference of sex was cut out with scissors. It seems probable that she had spoken to no man other than her father and her uncles. One can hardly be surprised at reading that her mental power was small, after being stunted in its growth in this fashion for eighteen years.

Napoleon sent as his proxy to Vienna Berthier, his trusted chief of staff. One can find nowhere any statement that the Austrians were pleased to see their princess standing side by side with a general whose latest acquired title was Prince of Wagram.

Perhaps as a sop to the national pride of Austria, Napoleon sent the bride he had not yet seen presents which have never been equalled in cost or magnificence. The trousseau he sent cost a hundred thousand francs; it included a hundred and fifty chemises each costing five pounds sterling, and enormous quantities of all other necessary linen. In addition he sent another hundred thousand francs' worth of lace and twelve dozen pairs of stockings at from one to three pounds sterling a pair. Dressing-table fittings and similar trifles cost nearly twenty thousand pounds, but all this expenditure was a mere trifle compared to the cost of the jewellery which Marie Louise received. The lowest estimate of this is placed at ten million francs—four hundred thousand pounds. Her dress allowance was to be over a thousand pounds a month.

Poor stupid Marie Louise might well fancy she was in Heaven. The daughter of an impoverished emperor, she had never possessed any jewellery other than a few corals and seed-pearls, and her wardrobe had been limited bŏth by her niggardly stepmother and by circumstances.

All her life she had been treated as a person of minor importance, but suddenly she found even her pride-ridden father regarding her with deference. Metternich and Schwartzenberg sought her favour. Her aunts and cousins clustered eagerly round her, anxious to share in the spoils. It certainly was a silver lining to the cloud of matrimony with an unknown.

Napoleon on his side was enraptured with the prospect. His meanness of soul is well displayed by his snobbish delight. He went to inordinate lengths in order to secure the approval of the great lady who had condescended to share his throne. He swept his palaces clear of anything which might remind his wife of her predecessor, and refurnished them with meticulous care. The fittings were standardized as far as possible, so that she might feel at once at home wherever she might choose to live; he even arranged a suite of rooms for her exactly like those she had lived in at Schrönbrunn. Napoleon gave his passion for organization full rein in matters of this kind, and without doubt he achieved a splendid success. "He was a good tenant, this Napoleon," said Louis XVIII., inspecting the Tuileries after the Restoration.

It was not merely her home that Napoleon adorned for Marie Louise, but even himself. For a space the green coat was laid aside, and he arrayed himself in a tunic stiff with embroidery. He tried to learn to waltz, and failed miserably. In everything he acted in a manner which amazed even those who had lived with him for years. No woman was half so excited over her first ball as was Napoleon over the prospect of marrying a Hapsburg.

He grew more and more excited as Marie Louise and her train journeyed across Germany and drew nearer and nearer. From every halting place despatches reached him in dozens. Marie Louise wrote to him, Caroline Murat (whom he had sent to welcome her) wrote to him, Berthier wrote to him, the ladies-in-waiting wrote to him, even the mayors of the towns passed through wrote to him. The officers who brought the letters were eagerly cross-questioned. The Emperor who, when on the brink of grand military events, would tell his attendants only to awaken him for bad news, passed his days waiting for his unknown bride in a fever of impatience.

At last he could bear it no longer. Napoleon was at Soissons, where the meeting had been arranged to take place, but, unable to wait, he rode forward post haste through pelting rain, with only Murat at his side. At Courcelles they met the Empress. At first the coachman was minded to drive past the two muddy figures who hailed him, but Napoleon made himself known, and clambered into the Imperial berline. He would brook not another moment's delay. The carriage pelted forward through all the towns where addresses of welcome were ready, where droves of damsels all in white were preparing to greet them, where banquets and fêtes were ready. They drove past Soissons, where a wonderful pavilion had been erected, in which the Imperial pair had expected to meet for the first time during a ceremony more pompous even than epoch-making Tilsit; they only stopped when they reached the palace of Compiegne, where, at nine o'clock at night, a hurried dinner was prepared by the astonished servants.

Even the dinner was cut short. Half-way through Napoleon asked Marie Louise a question; she blushed, and was unable to answer. It is to be doubted if she even knew what he was talking about. Napoleon turned to the Austrian envoy. "Her Majesty is doubtful," he said. "Is it not true that we are properly married?" The envoy hesitated. No one had expected that Napoleon would take the ceremony by proxy seriously; elaborate arrangements had been made for a further ceremony in Paris. But it was useless for the envoy to demur; Napoleon carried off Marie Louise to his own apartments, and breakfasted at her bedside next morning. Later his meanness of soul once more obtruded itself, when he hinted at his experiences to one of his friends.

If Napoleon was a parvenu among monarchs, he was at least able to show scoffers that his own royal ceremonies could put in the shade any similar display by thousand-year-old dynasties. At Marie Louise's coronation four queens bore her train.

Characteristically they tried to trip her up with it. Never before had the world beheld four queens bearing another woman's robes, and certainly never before had it seen anything parallel to the other exhibition.

When we come to see who these queens were, we shall appreciate the peculiar irony of the situation. First, there was the Queen of Spain, Joseph's wife, who was still angry about Napoleon's jilting of her sister Désirée, and who furthermore saw as a consequence of this marriage the probability of the arrival of a direct heir and the extinction of her husband's chances of the succession. Secondly came Caroline Murat, Queen of Naples, Napoleon's sister, violently jealous of Napoleon, of Marie Louise, and of everyone else. Third came the wife of Jerome Bonaparte, Catherine, Queen of Westphalia, whom Napoleon had torn from the arms of her betrothed to give to his loose-living young brother. The fourth was Hortense, Queen of Holland, whose mother Napoleon had just divorced in order to marry the

woman whose train Hortense was carrying.   Had
Marie Louise been capable of any unusual thought
whatever, she must have felt that she would be
safer entering a powder magazine than going up
the aisle of Nôtre Dame with those four viragoes
at her heels.

CHAPTER VII

SOME COURT DETAILS

ONCE bitten, twice shy. Napoleon had had one wife of whom doubtful stories had circulated. He would run no risk with the new one. Marie Louise had been strictly guarded all her life. Napoleon determined that in that respect he would substitute scorpions for her father's whips. No man was ever to be presented to his wife without his consent; under no circumstances whatever was she to be alone with a man at any time.

To achieve his object he revived all the court ceremony of the Soleil Monarque; he added a few oriental improvements of his own, and to see that his orders were carried out he surrounded Marie Louise with women who were the wives and sisters of his own generals, absolutely dependent on him and accustomed to military procedure.

The Austrian ladies who had attended on Marie Louise before her marriage were sent home, every single one of them, as soon as she crossed the frontier. Marie Louise bade good-bye there to the friends of a lifetime—Napoleon was risking nothing. As Dame d'Honneur and consequently first lady-in-waiting, Napoleon appointed the Duchess of Montebello, widow of the unfortunate Lannes, who had died fighting at Aspern against Marie Louise's father and an army commanded by Marie Louise's uncle. The

other important positions were filled in similar
fashion. Four "red women" were appointed,
whose duty was to be by the Empress's side night
and day, two on duty and two within call. Had
enough eunuchs been available, Napoleon would
probably have employed them. A seraglio would
have been quite in agreement with his estimation of
woman's constancy.

Considering that his court etiquette had to
recover from the citizen phase of the Revolution and
from the solemn, military stiffness of the Consulate,
Napoleon certainly succeeded remarkably well.
Where aides-de-camp sufficed in 1802, equerries were
necessary from 1804 onwards; the *maîtres d'hotel*
had to be replaced by chamberlains; the Empress's
friends had to be appointed ladies-in-waiting. Like
all reactions, this one went too far. The gaiety of
the Bourbon court was extinguished, and the devil-
may-care trifling of the Directory salons perished
equally miserably.

Napoleon himself was mainly responsible for this.
He was never good company in any sense of the
word. He had a remarkable gift for saying
unpleasant things in an unpleasant manner, and in
his presence the whole company was on tenterhooks,
wondering what was going to happen next. If a
lady had a snub nose, he said so; if a gentleman's
coat was shabby, he said so with fury, because it was
his pride to be the only shabby person present. If
rumours hinting at a lady's fall from virtue were in
circulation, he told her so at the top of his voice, and
demanded an explanation. When Napoleon quitted
his court he invariably left half the women in tears
and half the men in a rage. Then Talleyrand, Prince
of Benevento and Grand Chamberlain, would go
limping round from group to group, saying with his
twisted smile, "The Emperor commands you to be
amused."

While Josephine was Empress, this state of affairs was not so noticeable, for her dexterous tact soothed the smart caused by Napoleon's brusqueness, but under Marie Louise unbearable situations occurred again and again.

It must be admitted that the various parties at court made at least as dangerous a mixture as the constituents of gunpowder. To begin with, the members of the Imperial family itself were as jealous of each other as they could possibly be. Pauline, who was a mere Serene Highness, would grind her teeth when she had to address her sister Caroline as "Your Majesty." Caroline and the other Queens would rejoice openly because, being Queens, they were given armchairs when Napoleon's own mother had to be content with a stool. And they were one and all scheming for the succession in the event of Napoleon's fall.

Then there were still a few Republicans among the Princes and Dukes. One of the Marshals, compelled by Napoleon to be present at the solemn Mass which celebrated the Concordat, salved his conscience by swearing horribly throughout the ceremony, and, when asked by the First Consul how he had liked it, replied that it only needed to complete the picture the presence of the half million men who had died to uproot the system. Such men as these thought little of pushing in front of Serene Highnesses, or of laughing loudly when Pauline Bonaparte made the gesture which led to her banishment from court.

Then there were a few representatives of the old noblesse, to whom Napoleon, in his wholehearted snobbery, had offered large inducements to come to his court. These people regarded the ennobled barrel-coopers, smugglers and stable-boys with a mild but galling amusement. On one occasion Lannes, finding his path to the throne-room blocked

by these ci-devants, drew his sword and swore to cut
off the ears of the next person who impeded him.
It was naturally exasperating to the Marshals, who
had risen from the ranks in the course of twenty
campaigns, after receiving wounds in dozens, to find
these nobles given high positions purely on account
of their names. To make matters worse, there were
very lively suspicions that many of them had actually
borne arms against France as *émigrés*, in La Vendée,
on the Rhine, or in Italy. Yet even these considerations were of small account compared to the wrath
of the new nobility when they found that the old still
clung stubbornly together, and refused, apparently,
to admit even the existence of anyone outside the
Faubourg St. Germain.

The largest group at court was that of the new
nobility, but its superiority of numbers was dis-
counted by the violent jealousies of its individual
members. The maxim which guided Napoleon in
his dealings with his subordinates was, apparently,
"Divide et impera." He set his generals and
ministers by the ears until there was not one of them
who had not some cherished hatred for another.
Davout hated Berthier, Lannes hated Bessières,
Ney hated Masséna, Fouché hated them all, Savary
hated Talleyrand ; and the resultant bickerings were
incessant. At court this was merely undignified ;
in the field, as was proved twenty times over in the
Peninsular War, it was positively dangerous. It
might be thought that Napoleon, with inexhaustible
funds and domains at his disposal, and unlimited
princely titles in his gift, could have satisfied them
all. But that was where the trouble began.
Napoleon could not give them all they desired, as
otherwise (such was the condition of the Empire)
they would have nothing to fight for. There were
glaring examples of this. When Masséna had been
made a prince, and had accumulated wealth and

glory past calculation, he deteriorated hopelessly.
He failed badly in the Busaco campaign of 1810-11,
and sank promptly into an effete degeneracy at the
age of fifty-five. No, Napoleon could not afford to
give his Marshals all they desired, and in consequence
jealousies and friction increased unbearably.

With the junior officers the difficulties were just
as great. Brutes like Vandamme, aristocrats like
Belliard and Ségur, rakes like Lasalle and fools like
Grouchy, were all mingled together. What was
worse was that generals and diplomats of subject
states necessarily came into contact with them also.
It must have been maddening for the Prussian,
Von Yorck, to hear Vandamme discoursing on the
plunder he had acquired in Silesia in 1806, or for
Schwartzenburg, the Austrian, to hear Lasalle
boasting of his successes among the ladies of Vienna
during the Austerlitz campaign.

But for a whole year, beginning in 1810,
Napoleon in spite of these difficulties was supremely
happy. There was peace all over the Continent,
and the Continental system seemed at last to be on
the point of success, for England's finances were
undoubtedly shaken. So short was gold in England
that Wellington in the Peninsula rarely had enough
for his needs, and the Portuguese and Spanish
subsidies were heavily in arrears. Masséna with
a hundred thousand men had plunged into the fog
of guerilla warfare on the Tagus, and everyone was
confidently expecting to hear of the fall of Lisbon
and the expulsion of the English from Portugal.

Meanwhile, Napoleon was savouring the delights
of respectable married life. With his nineteen-year-
old wife he indulged in all sorts of innocent pleasures,
riding, hunting, practical joking, theatricals. He so
far forgot himself as to *tutoyer* his Imperial bride in
the presence of his whole Court, and the mighty
nobles (who never indulged in such behaviour even

in the intimacy of their wives' boudoirs) were astonished to hear the Emperor and Empress exchanging " thees " and " thous."

Napoleon gave up hours of his precious time to his wife, waited patiently when she was late for an appointment (Josephine was never guilty of such an offence) and generally acted the devoted husband to the life. For a whole year he was faithful to Marie Louise, a feat which he never achieved before or after until St. Helena. And as the months rolled by and hope changed to certainty his devotion grew greater still.

For the birth of the child the most elaborate preparations were made. Some time before he was born Mme. de Montesquieu was named Governess of the Children of France, a healthy Normandy girl who was in the same condition as the Empress was secured as prospective wet nurse and kept under strict surveillance (her own child died when it was taken from her, but that is not usually recorded), and all France waited in a hush of expectation.

Once again Napoleon was risking nothing. He was going to leave no possible foundation for rumours to the effect that the child was not his, or was not Marie Louise's. Napoleon Francis Joseph Charles was born in the presence of the four doctors, Dubois, Corvisart, Bourdier and Yvan; of the Duchess of Montebello, dame d'honneur; of Mme. de Luçay, dame d'atours; of Mme. de Montesquieu, Governess of the Children of France; of six premières dames de chambre; of five women of inferior rank, and of two filles de garde-robe. Cambacères, Duke of Parma and Archchancellor of the Empire, was present in an ante-room, and should have witnessed the birth even if he did not; Berthier, Prince of Neufchâtel and Wagram, was in attendance on Napoleon, and also may have witnessed it, while immediately after the birth all the other Grand

Dignitaries of the Empire and the representatives of all the friendly countries of Europe were paraded through the room. Napoleon had ordered Corvisart, whose nerve was giving way under the strain of the business, to treat Marie Louise like a bourgeois wife, but he hardly practised what he preached. The birth took three days; it certainly seemed a good omen for this scrap of humanity to keep all these dozens of people with high-sounding titles waiting for seventy-two consecutive hours.

After an anxious ten minutes the young Napoleon showed signs of life; he had at first appeared to be dead, and brandy had to be given him and he had to be discreetly smacked before he would cry. But he did so at length, and Napoleon announced to the waiting dignitaries, "It is a King of Rome." The guns fired a salute to inform the expectant crowds; twenty-one guns were to herald the birth of a daughter; one hundred a son. At the twenty-second gun a storm of cheers arose. More than forty years after, a ceremony almost identical announced the birth of an equally ill-fated son to another Emperor of the French.

Thus the wish of Napoleon's heart was fulfilled. For the moment he disregarded all the counter-balancing disadvantages and revelled in the possession of an heir. He cared nothing at the time for the fact that the doctors forbade the Empress to have the much desired second son to inherit the crown of Italy; it was nothing to him that Bavaria, Holland, Wurtemberg and Saxony at once became restless at seeing their period of thraldom indefinitely prolonged; he hardly cared that Masséna had come miserably back from Portugal, with a ruined army, baulked irretrievably by Wellington at Torres Vedras, so that the "running sore" of the Peninsular campaign was reopened. He flung away his last chance of going in person to end the business, merely to remain by the side of the wife and child of whom he was so proud.

But despite his pride, he still left nothing to chance. Attendance on Marie Louise was maintained as strictly as before; an unauthorized presentation to the Empress by the Duchess of Montebello of some relation of hers called forth a tornado of wrath from the Emperor. The surveillance was redoubled when Napoleon left for the Russian campaign, although he paid her a compliment which had never been paid to Josephine—he appointed her Regent. Poor, silly Marie Louise, three years after being an insignificant princess, found herself Empress of the French, Queen of Italy and Regent of half Europe!

Her august husband nevertheless saw fit to have the Empress-Queen-Regent spied upon by a scullion, who sent him weekly reports, fantastically spelt on blotched and smeared kitchen paper! Nothing else is necessary to prove how utterly lacking in decent instincts was the victor of Austerlitz.

The action was typical of many. Perhaps Napoleon was right; everyone knows how readily autocracy becomes bureaucracy when the autocrat ceases to supervise his subordinates adequately; but not even the Second Empire nor Russia at the beginning of the twentieth century could show so many spies and counter-spies, police and counter-police and counter counter-police as did the First Empire. Secret delation flourished, and the prisons were full of people who had been arbitrarily cast into gaol without even a form of trial. Napoleon wished to know everything that was going on; not the least stray fragment of tittle-tattle came amiss to him. Consequently his regular police developed an organization which spread its tentacles into every avenue of life. Fouché, Minister of Police, could boast of having an agent in every drawing-room and

kitchen in the Empire. But then Napoleon feared
that Fouché would distort for his own purposes the
reports of the agents when making his own report
to Napoleon. Since Fouché was Fouché such a
thing was not unlikely. So Napoleon had a second
and independent police system making similar
reports to another minister. Yet even when
Fouché was at last got rid of, and packed off as
His Excellency the Governor of Rome (and later
Dalmatia); even when Savary, "the man who
would kill his own father if Napoleon ordered it,"
was in charge of the police affairs the dual police
system was still adhered to. And besides these,
Napoleon had spies of his own, working quite
independently, reporting direct to himself, and he
placed these not only in the two original police
systems, but everywhere where they could keep an
eye on those in high places. His royal brothers
were surrounded with them; they were to be found
in the secretariats of all the ministers; and since
payment was largely by results, and they had to
justify their existence somehow, it is not surprising
that they brought forward trumped-up charges,
suborned perjury, and generally acted as typical
Continental agents-provocateurs. But all this
elaborate system failed to gain the least hint of
the Mallet conspiracy, which came so near to pulling
down the Empire in the autumn of 1812.

There were opportunities enough for conspiracy,
goodness knows. Bourbonists and Republicans,
Bonapartists and anarchists, all sought to keep or
to acquire power. The Murats, the Beauharnais,
the various Bonaparte brothers and even Bernadotte, were all scheming for the succession or the
regency, while intertwining among all this was the
more legitimate scheming of the various European
powers, whose secret agents were equally active
throughout the Empire. There is small room for

wonder that after a dozen years of this frantic merry-go-round the French people accepted the Bourbon restoration quietly, lest worse befall.

Yet all this does not excuse Napoleon for spying on his wife; for that the only justification lies in the event. How many times has Napoleon been rated for saying that adultery is a matter of opportunity? But his wife apparently did her best to prove him right. In 1814 the Empire was falling, and Napoleon's abdication was evidently inevitable. One thing alone raised him to an equality with hereditary monarchs, and that was the fact that he had married the daughter of the greatest of them all. They might exile General Bonaparte, but would they dare to exile along with him the Emperor of Austria's daughter? Besides, in Marie Louise's keeping was the young Napoleon. To allow him to accompany his mother into exile with his father was simply to court disaster.

At first the prospect seemed dark for the Allies. Marie Louise stood firm, refused to be parted either from her son or from her husband, and generally acted the devoted wife to the life. In this dilemma the Allies appealed to the most cunning and cold-hearted of all their agents—Metternich, who for thirty years was to hold Europe in the hollow of his hand. Metternich was the cynic magnificent, without belief in the constancy of any man or woman born. In that self-seeking age his opinions were largely justified. Metternich plunged adroitly into the affair. He must have known a great deal about the mentality of feeble-minded women, seeing that one of his boasts was that he never had fewer than three mistresses at a time. He selected an agent whom no one at first sight would have believed to be of any use, but who turned out to be extremely valuable. If Neipperg was a knave, he was at least the knave of trumps. He was an elderly one-eyed diplomat,

GRAF VON NEIPPERG

a count and a general in the Austrian army, with a good record behind him. He justified Metternich's choice remarkably quickly, and while His Imperial, Royal and Apostolic Majesty looked on and applauded this prostitution of his daughter, he wormed his way into Marie Louise's affections, so that by the time Napoleon was deposited in Elba, Marie Louise's second child (whose engendering Corvisart had so strictly forbidden) was expected in a few months' time, while her first was under lock and key at Schönbrunn, deprived of all his French friends and attendants, and started on the unhappy life which was to end sixteen years later in consumption, despair and death.

To Napoleon's credit be it recorded that never by word or deed did he hint at this horrible desertion. All the rest of his life he spoke of Marie Louise with affection and respect, and had he had his way, Marie Louise would have been Regent of the French during the minority of Napoleon II.

Marie Louise lived happily for another thirty years. The Allies rewarded her adultery by giving her the sovereignty of Parma for life, and there she lived with Neipperg, whom she married morganatically as soon as Napoleon was dead. For a long time she bore him one child a year, and the Emperor of Austria, with great consideration, made all of them, illegitimate and morganatic alike, princes and princesses of the Empire. No sooner was Neipperg dead than she contracted another morganatic marriage with a person of even lowlier degree. When she was expelled from her duchy by the rising of 1831, she was restored by Austrian bayonets, and she died at length a year before the far more serious rising of 1848. She never saw her first-born child after 1815 until he was on his death-bed in 1832.

The unfortunate Louise of Tuscany, who

E

married and then deserted the Crown Prince of
Saxony, tells us that to her, as to all the other
Hapsburg princesses, Marie Louise's career was
held up as a shining example of the fortune which
attended good girls who did just what the head of
the family, the Emperor, told them.   But the
Emperor of Austria, since he had nothing to gain
by it, did not condone the adultery of this particular
Archduchess.

CHAPTER VIII

THE GREATEST PALADIN

IN the course of his military career Napoleon found he needed three different kinds of subordinate officers. First, he wanted men of supreme courage and vigour in action, whose other talents need not be more than mediocre. These he could keep under his own hand until the decisive moment arrived, and could then let loose, confident that they would complete the work which his strategic achievements had begun. Of this type, Ney, Augereau and Oudinot were examples.

Then he needed a few generals who combined initiative and resource along with their tactical talents. On these he could rely to execute minor strategical movements, knowing that their tactical skill would help them to sustain any difficulties into which they might fall until the perfection of his strategical arrangements helped them out. The supreme example of this type was Lannes the irreplaceable.

Besides these, Napoleon needed one or two men who could combine all the qualities necessary to a good general, so that he could entrust to them the supreme command of the minor theatres of war. To be a good general, a man must possess strategical skill, tactical skill and administrative ability, as well as the personality to ensure that his ideas are carried out. But to satisfy Napoleon's jealousy, such a

general in the Imperial army had to have another
quality—he had to be a man who would never allow
his thoughts to wander in the direction of obtaining
the throne for himself. If Napoleon could have
found three men with all these qualifications he
could very possibly have maintained his Empire,
since they would have assured to him the safety of
Italy, Spain and Poland. But there was only one
of these Admirable Crichtons available, and that
was Davout. Under Davout Poland and North
Germany were held strongly for the Empire. In
Italy Eugène de Beauharnais, by the aid of powerful
common-sense, high ideals and capable subordinates,
was fairly successful, but in Spain there was nothing
but shame and disaster. Masséna failed badly; so
did Marmont; Joseph Bonaparte and his Major-
General, Jourdan, were worse than useless; Soult
and Suchet made a fair show, but could not rise
superior to the handicap of circumstances. Another
Davout might have saved Spain for the Empire, but
there was only one Davout.

Davout is the ideal type of the man who combines ability with a sense of duty. In many ways
he reminds one of Wellington. He was the scion
of an old noble and military family of Burgundy,
and was born a year later than Napoleon. He
passed through the military college, and received his
commission in 1789, just before the Revolution.
The loss of many officers through emigration gave
him rapid promotion. He was a colonel in 1791
(at the age of twenty-one!) and a brigadier-general
two years later. Already he had attracted attention
by the stern discipline he maintained (discipline
was hardly the most noticeable feature of the
Revolutionary armies) and Napoleon, realizing his
ability, included him in his army after Campo
Formo. He went to Egypt as one of Desaix'
brigadiers, and returned with the same general in

1800. After Marengo and the treaty of Luneville, Napoleon gave him employment suitable to his talents, and appointed him to the command of the 3rd Corps of the Army of the Ocean. A marshalate followed in 1804. As commander of the 3rd Corps Davout began to build up the wonderful reputation which he later enjoyed. There was no other force in the Grand Army which could rival the 3rd Corps for discipline, for marching capacity, for fighting capacity, and for perfection of equipment.

The 3rd Corps was to Napoleon what the Numidians were to Hannibal, the Tenth Legion to Cæsar, the archers to Edward III., the Light Division to Wellington—they were the men who could be trusted most nearly to achieve the impossible.

At Austerlitz Davout was called upon to sustain the attack of practically the whole of the Austro-Russian army, and he and the 3rd Corps clung doggedly on to the difficult country round the lakes for hour after hour while Napoleon developed his attack on the heights of Pratzen. Before Austerlitz Napoleon had declared that an ordinary victory would be of no use to him; on the morning of the battle he called upon his men for a " *coup de tonnerre.*" But for Davout Austerlitz would have been at best an " ordinary victory."

The next campaign, that of Jena, was marked by the failure of Napoleon's intelligence arrangements and by confusion in his strategical arrangements. But it was also marked by the most sweeping success Napoleon ever gained. He himself with most of the Grand Army fought and routed half the Prussian army at Jena. On the same day Davout, with a single corps, fought and routed the other half at Auerstädt. Single-handed Davout sustained the attack of an army of twice his strength; he beat off Blucher and the furious Prussian squadrons; he

counter-attacked without hesitation; he called for
efforts of which few troops could have been capable,
and finally he flung the enemy back in utter disorder.

The battle was more than a mere tactical success.
Without Davout's victory the pursuit after Jena
would never have become historic.   In fact Napoleon
refrained from pursuit until he had heard from
Davout.   Well he might, indeed.   Had Davout
been beaten, Napoleon must have swung aside to
face the victors, who would have been menacing his
flank; Bernadotte's corps would have been isolated
and in serious peril, and there would have been no
chance of close pursuit of Hohenlohe's force.   This
would have had time to rally; the stern Prussian
discipline would have knitted it once more together;
it might have made a good defence of the line of
the Elbe; the Russians might have arrived in time
to save Berlin; there would perhaps have been no
Friedland, and no Tilsit.

The stout little bald-pated man who commanded
the 3rd Corps changed the face of Europe at
Auerstädt.

Davout brought his corps through blizzards and
across marshes to save the situation at Eylau; it was
his opportune arrival and bold counsel which saved
Napoleon from a grave tactical reverse, with probable
serious consequences.

After Friedland Napoleon needed, as has already
been said, a man of iron to hold down the north
while he attended to the south.   He made the only
possible choice in Davout.

It would seem curious to us nowadays to hear
that a general had made his fortune while in command; what a storm of rage would be aroused if
anyone were to suggest that a modern English
general had acquired three or four hundred thousand
pounds while commanding in France!   But apparently under the First Republic and First Empire it

was the usual practice for all officers of high rank to plunder for their own hands, and to make enormous fortunes out of perquisites. Davout was the only exception, but Napoleon saw that he did not suffer on account of his singular disinterestedness, and heaped wealth upon him.

Another peculiar distinction which he gave him was the title of Duke of Auerstädt. When, about the beginning of 1808, Napoleon first began to bestow titles of honour, as distinct from titles of sovereignty, he acted upon a very definite plan. No one was to receive a title which did not enhance the glory of the Emperor. The less famous Marshals received ducal fiefs in Italy; Macdonald was made Duke of Tarentum, Mortier Duke of Treviso, Bessières Duke of Istria. With the title the Marshals received the fief with some show of sovereignty, but they were allowed—encouraged, in fact—to sell their sovereignties to the Empire as soon as received.

The more famous Marshals took their titles from the battles in which they had taken part; Lannes was made Duke of Montebello, Ney Duke of Elchingen. Lefebvre, whose reputation for republicanism Napoleon repeatedly employed to hallmark his own actions, was created Duke of Dantzic. Soult strove to obtain for himself the title of Duke of Austerlitz, but Napoleon put the idea impatiently aside. He wished to reserve the glory of Austerlitz entirely for himself, and Soult had to be content with the title of Duke of Dalmatia, which set him in the lower class of Marshal. But Napoleon's jealousy went further than this. He did not want to give anyone a title derived from a battle which had not been fought under his own direction. He forced the title of Duke of Rivoli upon Masséna, although that Marshal had to his credit the far greater achievements of Zurich and Genoa. When it was suggested to him that it would be a kindly action to make the unhappy, neglected Jourdan Duke of Fleurus, he replied " Never! I might as well make him King of France at once."

To this rule Napoleon only made two exceptions. One was Kellermann, whom he made Duke of Valmy, but by now Kellermann was too old (he was seventy-three) to be any danger, while Valmy was a landmark in French history. The other was Davout.

The Duke of Auerstädt had before him in 1807 a task which would give his sternness and devotion to duty free play. He had command of at least a hundred thousand men. For the support of these he received not a sou from the French Government —everything, pay, provisions and equipment, had to be wrung from the wretched countries in which they were in garrison. From Prussia Davout had to grind the enormous indemnity which Napoleon had imposed. In Westphalia he had to see that Jerome Bonaparte did not make too big a fool of himself. He had to keep a sharp eye upon the movements of Austria. Besides all this, he had to govern the infant Grand Duchy of Warsaw, where he had simultaneously to assure the Poles that an independent kingdom of Poland would shortly be set up, and the Russians and Austrians that an independent kingdom of Poland would never be set up.

And yet he succeeded. Throughout northern central Europe he built himself up a reputation as the justest brute in Christendom. His army was well fed and well equipped, but he did his best to make the burden as light as possible. He saw that Napoleon's outrageous demands of Prussia were complied with, but at the same time he was not unnecessarily harsh. He sent Polish regiments to fight in Spain (at Poland's expense) while he kept French troops about Warsaw (also at Poland's expense), but he managed to persuade the Poles

that such a proceeding was just. He carried out
Napoleon's orders both in the spirit and to the letter,
but after that he made enormous and successful
efforts to minimize the damage done. What would
a second Davout have done in Spain?

Early in 1809 his proceedings were interrupted.
Austria, undaunted by the conference of Erfurt, and
inspirited by the success of the Spaniards, was on
the move again. Davout had to concentrate his
enormous force on the upper Danube as rapidly as
possible, with a weather eye lifting in case of a
further effort by Prussia, and, once there, he had
to weld his troops once more into divisions and army
corps. From all quarters other troops were being
rushed to the scene of action, and in command of
them all was the hesitating Berthier. Napoleon,
with his hands full with the Spanish muddle, tried
to direct operations from Paris as long as possible.
The natural result was that when the Emperor
arrived at headquarters he found his army divided
and in an apparently hopeless position, with the
skilful and resolute Archduke Charles thrusting
enormous forces between the dislocated wings.
Only a supreme effort could save the situation, but
the situation was saved. Napoleon gathered together
Lannes, Vandamme and Masséna, and hurled them
forward. He called upon Davout to achieve the
impossible, and make a flank march of thirty miles
while in actual contact with superior forces. The
impossible was achieved. Davout brought his men
safely through, to gain along with the other forces
the shattering victory of Eckmühl.

Davout's performance is practically unique in
military history. A year or two later the disastrous
possibilities of a flank march were thoroughly demon-
strated at Salamanca, where Marmont, who prided
himself upon his tactical ability, was utterly routed in
an hour's fighting by Wellington. Marmont had

good troops, and his army was as nearly as possible
equal to Wellington's, but this did not save him.
Davout's force was partly composed of new troops,
and of disaffected allies, while his opponents were
nearly twice his strength.   Only the most consum-
mate daring combined with the maximum of vigilance
and skill could have saved Davout, but Davout was
saved.   The title of Prince of Eckmühl which
Napoleon bestowed upon him was well deserved.

The next outstanding incident in the campaign
was Napoleon's first defeat in the open field.   He
dared just a little too much in attempting to cross
a broad river in the face of a powerful opponent, with
the result that he was beaten back with frightful loss.
Lannes was mortally wounded; the bridges by which
the army had crossed were broken before Davout's
turn came to pass over.

For a while the Empire tottered.   A prompt
offensive on the part of the Archduke Charles might
have overthrown it, but his army, too, had been hard
hit, and he delayed.   Napoleon's frantic exertions
turned the scale in the end.   He claimed Aspern as
a victory, and so skilfully did he make his claim that
for a time he was believed throughout Europe.
Masséna was created Prince of Essling, to conceal
the defeat—in much the same way as the Earl of
Chatham might have been made Duke of Walcheren
in the same year.   The army of Italy, under
Eugene, Macdonald and Marmont outmarched their
opponents, and arrived in time to enable the
Emperor to cast the die once more.

He passed the Danube a little lower down than
at his previous attempt, turned the Austrian position,
and fought the battle of Wagram on practically equal
terms.   It was evenly contested, too.   Masséna on
the left was beaten back until the flank was nearly
turned; Bernadotte's Saxon corps was repulsed in
terrible disorder, and the French reserves were drawn

EUGENE DE BEAUHARNAIS
(VICEROY OF ITALY ; PRINCE DE VENISE)

in at an alarming rate. A hundred French guns, massed in the centre, battered the Austrian line, and Macdonald led his corps, formed in a gigantic square, against the gap. But he suffered terribly from the Austrian artillery, and his men left the ranks in thousands. In the end, it was Davout on the right who won the battle for the French, for he turned the Austrian left and began to roll up their line; the Austrians fell sullenly back. It was a defeat, not a disaster, but the Austrians sued for peace immediately afterwards.

After Wagram Davout went back to his old post in the north. Month by month the position grew more and more difficult, as the topsy-turvy finances of the Grand Duchy of Warsaw verged nearer to bankruptcy, and the spirit of nationality grew in Prussia. But there was never a hint of open rebellion as long as the bald-headed little man was at the head of affairs; the Tugendbund might plot in secret; English agents might stir up trouble at every opportunity; Blucher might fume and Alexander might plan, but Davout's grip was never loosened.

At last, after three years, came the Russian campaign. Half a million Frenchmen and allies came thronging forward to the Niemen. A hundred thousand of these men were under Davout's command, and, with Napoleon's new supply arrangements breaking down at once, they had to plunder in order to live. Prussia was left behind secretly raging, and the doomed army pressed forward over the barren plains of Lithuania. Everything seemed to go wrong. The half-trained levies could not perform the feats of marching which had gained such marvellous successes at Ulm and after Jena; the Marshals wrangled among themselves; while Napoleon, angered by the failure of his plans, dealt out reprimands right and left until the irritation became almost unbearable. Jerome Bonaparte,

King of Westphalia, was placed under Davout's command in consequence of his blundering, but he could not endure such a state of affairs, threw up his command, and went back to the softer delights of his palace at Cassel.

With Moscow almost in sight, the Russians delivered battle. Napoleon's powers were fast waning, and he paid no heed to Davout's urgent pleading that he should be allowed to turn their left. At Wagram he had exclaimed, " You will see Davout gain another battle for me," but at Borodino he had forgotten this. The battle resolved itself into a series of horribly costly frontal assaults, and the victors lost as heavily as their opponents. There followed five weeks' useless delay in Moscow; Napoleon waited for Alexander to plead for terms, and Alexander refused to consider the matter as long as a Frenchman remained on Russian soil. No course was open to the French except retreat, and retreat they did. There is no need to describe in detail that exhausted famished army crawling across the Russian plains; sufficient to say that of the half million men who had advanced in 1812 hardly thirty thousand remained to rally on the Oder in 1813.

Napoleon left them as soon as hope was lost. He tore across Europe from Smorgoni to Paris in the depth of winter with hardly a stop, bent on making a last effort to save his Empire. Murat was left in command, but Murat flinched from his task. Three weeks of command were enough for him, and then he said he was ill. Ill or not, he travelled from Posen to Naples in a fortnight, in January weather.

Somehow Davout and Ney and Eugène de Beauharnais held the wretched Grand Army together until Napoleon's return, and then Davout was sent off to hold down Northern Germany once more. It was a task which might have daunted anybody. Prussia was ablaze with hatred of Napoleon, and

Prussian troops were swarming forward to the attack.
The citizens of the Hanseatic towns, ruined by the
Continental system, and bankrupted by Napoleon's
requisitions, were in a state of sullen rebellion.
Davout's troops consisted merely of invalids, cripples
and raw levies, while the loyalty of most of them
was to be doubted. Bernadotte, once a Marshal
of France, was leading his Swedes against his old
countrymen. Benningsen with a Russian army
advanced to the attack. But Davout's grip was upon
Hamburg, and it was a grip which nothing could
break. He held on through the summer of 1813,
while the armistice of Pleissvitz gave hope of relief.
He held on through the autumn, while Austria joined
the ranks of Napoleon's enemies. The victory of
Dresden was followed by the defeats of the Katzbach,
of Kulm, of Gross Beeren, of Dennewitz, and finally
by the complete disaster of Leipzig, but Davout still
held on to Hamburg. Provisions began to fail, the
populace broke into insurrection; it was known that
the Allies were over the Rhine, that Napoleon was
carrying on a hopeless struggle in France itself.
Marmont, Mortier, Ney, in turn deserted, but
Davout still held on to Hamburg. It was not until
the end of April, when the Bourbons were once more
on the throne of France, and a Bourbon general was
sent to take command, that he relaxed his grip.
Half his army had died during the horrors of the
siege, enormous offers had been made to him for his
submission, the famished inhabitants had implored
him to surrender, but he had allowed nothing to interfere with his fulfilment of his duty.

The Bourbons tried to have him shot for this on
his return, but such a feat was beyond their power.
Thus he was not asked, nor did he ask to take the
oath of allegiance.

On Napoleon's return from Elba Davout was the
only Marshal who could join him without staining

his honour. Marmont stayed by the Bourbons, for
fear of the consequences of his surrender of Paris;
Macdonald and St. Cyr, Oudinot and Victor, held to
their oaths. Ney flagrantly broke his word to serve
his old Emperor once more; Masséna, as was to be
expected, tried to keep a middle course. Davout
was the one man free from the Bourbon taint, and in
consequence Napoleon had to leave him behind as
Governor of Paris and Minister of War to hold
France quiet during the Waterloo campaign.

Could it have been otherwise, Waterloo might
well have been a victory for France. We can picture
Davout in command of the left wing in the advance
over the Sambre. In place of Ney's bungled staff
work and haphazard arrangements, there would have
been a prompt and orderly movement. The columns
would have been kept closed up, instead of straggling
for miles. Davout's accurate, lengthy reports would
have kept Napoleon clearly informed as to the situation. A prompt attack on the morning of the 16th
of June at Quatre Bras would have cleared the air
effectively, and d'Erlon, instead of wasting his
strength in marching and counter-marching, could
have been employed to much better advantage at
Ligny. Ney's position at Quatre Bras was, as a
matter of fact, very like Davout's at Auerstädt eleven
years before. Davout succeeded at Auerstädt; Ney
failed at Quatre Bras. With Davout in command
of the left wing in the Waterloo campaign, the
history of the world might have been different.

At Waterloo, when the cavalry was dashing itself
to pieces on the English squares, Napoleon is said to
have cried, " Oh, for one hour of Murat." Murat
by that time would not have made an atom of difference. The destiny of France had been decided two
days before at Quatre Bras. One hour of Davout
would have been worth fifty hours of Murat.

After Waterloo had been lost and won, for a few

days it was the Prince of Eckmühl who ruled France. He pulled the army together, and thereby saved Napoleon's life, for he managed to stave off the Prussian army while Napoleon fled to Rochefort. But with the return of the Bourbons he sank into oblivion, and died of pneumonia eight years afterwards almost unnoticed.

Such was the end of the one great officer of Napoleon's whose honour had never been sullied, who had always done his duty, and who had never failed. His enemies hated him as well as feared him; his friends feared him as well as trusted him. His one aim in life was to do his duty; in this aim he stood almost alone in his age, and in its achievement he stood quite alone.

CHAPTER IX

MORE PALADINS

WHEN the Marshalate was inaugurated, the first list afforded many opportunities for dissatisfaction, both among those included and those excluded.

Men like Macdonald and St. Cyr, of high reputation and undoubted talents, found themselves ignored for political reasons, while giants of the Republican armies like Masséna found that Napoleon's family feeling had given comparatively unknown men like Murat seniority over them. Masséna's curt reply to congratulations on his new appointment was " Yes, one of fourteen," and it must indeed have been galling to him to have Bessières, Moncey and other nonentities raised to a rank equal to his own.

For in 1804 Masséna towered in achievement head and shoulders above all other French soldiers, with the exception of Napoleon. He was of Italian extraction (many people said Jewish-Italian, and hinted that Masséna was a euphonized version of Manasseh), and he had served fourteen years in Louis XVI.'s regiment of Italian mercenaries. Quitting the army, he had plunged into the various shady employments of the Côte d'Azur. Smuggling by land and by sea, coast trading, wine-dealing, fruit-selling, he tried his hand at them all, mainly successfully.

But with the revolution came his chance. In two years he was general of division, and he actually had under his orders at Toulon a certain Napoleon Bonaparte. For two campaigns Masséna was the life and soul of the army of the Riviera; Dumerbion, Schérer, and even Moreau turned to him for counsel. Then suddenly Barras sent Napoleon as commander-in-chief in 1796. It is perhaps the greatest tribute to Napoleon's personality that as a young man of twenty-six he was able to compel obedience from a crowd of generals, many years his senior both in age and experience. Masséna yielded place to him grudgingly, but Napoleon found a golden salve for his injured amour-propre. The campaign of Italy laid the foundations of the enormous fortune which Masséna later built up. Every general pillaged and peculated right and left in those two memorable years. Napoleon himself was moderate; his fortune at the end of 1797 only amounted to about two hundred thousand pounds sterling; Masséna and Augereau acquired about half a million each.

But if they could steal, these men could also fight. Masséna was the supreme master of tactics, and it was his division which at that time was given the most difficult tasks. Battle followed battle, Montenotte, Mondovi, Lodi, Lonato, Castiglione, Mantua, Arcola, Rivoli, until at last Austria succumbed; and by that time, what with gold and glory, the generals of the army of Italy were Napoleon's slaves.

Napoleon had served another purpose, too, in enriching Masséna, for his wealth kept him quiet while Napoleon was in Egypt. In 1798 the Directory made a curious blunder. Their army of Rome, maddened by the peculations of generals and commissaries, which left the men half starved and in rags, broke out into mutiny. The man who was sent to quell them was Masséna! The mutiny naturally redoubled in intensity, and Masséna was compelled to give up his command. But at once more congenial work was given him. Another coalition had

F

declared war upon France, and the Archduke Charles
in Germany and Suvaroff in Italy were gaining success
after success. Masséna was sent to command in
Switzerland, the last buttress of France. Upon him
depended all the hopes of the Republic, and well
he justified the Republic's confidence. He clung
on desperately, holding back immensely superior
numbers. At last the Aulic Council at Vienna
blundered more badly than usual, and Masséna
grasped at the opportunity, as if it had been a money-
bag. He flung himself upon Korsakoff at Zurich,
and practically destroyed his army. Suvaroff, marching over the St. Gothard, only escaped the same fate
by a desperate march along the wildest paths of
Switzerland. France was saved in the same hour as
Napoleon seized the reins of the Government.

By varied cajolery Napoleon next prevailed upon
Masséna to take command of the army of Italy, and
to hold back the Austrian army while he himself
organized the army of reserve. Napoleon had assured
Masséna that the army of Italy was in good condition,
and that supplies and reinforcements would be sent
him in abundance, but as soon as Masséna arrived
he found how little trust could be placed in the
First Consul's word. The men were starving and
dispirited, and they were attacked by vastly superior
forces. Somehow Masséna held them together, but
he was forced back into Genoa and closely besieged.
For the troops there was some sort of food, hair-
powder and cocoa mainly, but for the inhabitants
there was—*nothing*. For nine weeks Masséna held
out. The troops died in hundreds by the sword,
by disease, by starvation; the inhabitants died in
thousands, and their bodies littered the streets. The
Austrian prisoners who were taken starved to death
in the hulks in the harbour. No wonder that Masséna
said that after the siege he had not one hair left
which was not white on his whole body.

At last surrender was necessary. Napoleon had promised him prompt relief, but the relief never came. Day by day Masséna had listened for the thunder of his guns in the near-by Apennines, but it had never reached his ears. The capitulation was signed, and the French marched out. But while Masséna had been clinging to Genoa, Napoleon's army was swinging over the Alps. Ten days after the surrender of Genoa, Marengo gave Italy once more to the French.

To Masséna, covered with glory, Napoleon gave the command of the army of Italy on his own return to Paris; but the arrangement did not long endure. Within two months Masséna's avarice had got the better of him, and he was removed from his command and placed upon half-pay on account of his sharp practice.

This retirement endured for four years, but in the Austerlitz campaign Masséna received the command-in-chief in Italy. If he accomplished little here, at least he prevented the enemy from achieving any success, and after Austerlitz and the treaty of Presburg he was sent to conquer Naples for Joseph Bonaparte. The campaign was a mere military promenade, but it ended, as did so many of Masséna's commands, in his compulsory resignation on account of his illicit money-making. On this occasion Napoleon improved on his previous practice, and confiscated over a hundred thousand pounds which Masséna had accumulated in a Livornese bank.

Once again Napoleon summoned Masséna to his aid in 1807, and at Pultusk and Friedland Masséna divided the laurels with Lannes and Ney. But it was the Wagram campaign which brought him the greatest glory, as it did also to Davout. At Eckmühl Masséna performed the turning movement which gained the victory after Davout's holding

attack. At Essling it was Masséna who held the
reeling French line together until darkness brought
relief. At Wagram Masséna, crippled just before
by a fall from his horse, led his corps in a coach drawn
by white horses, the mark for all the enemy's guns.
Small wonder was it that the end of the campaign
found Masséna both Duke of Rivoli and Prince of
Essling, with a pension of twenty thousand pounds a
year in addition to his pay, his perquisites and his
enormous savings.

But this was the zenith of Masséna's fame; it was
to reach its nadir immediately afterwards. Masséna
had lived hard all his life; he had spared himself no
more than he had spared his men, and in addition
he had at intervals indulged in unbridled debauchery.
By 1810 Masséna was an old, worn-out, satiated man,
although he was only fifty-five years of age. All he
wished to do was to retire and live in peace, but
Napoleon was at his wits' end to find someone who
could be trusted in Spain. Masséna found the command thrust upon him, and he was forced to accept.
Then followed the blundering campaign of Torres
Vedras. Blunders in the choice of route, blunders in
the attack at Busaco, blunders at Torres Vedras, and
finally, in 1811, the crowning blunder of Fuentes
d'Onoro.

These blunders might have been foreseen;
Masséna was old and feeble; he knew nothing of
Spain; he took women with him on the campaign;
his corps commanders were Ney, Junot and Reynier,
all men of hot temper and inferior talent; while
opposed to him was the inflexible Wellington with
his incomparable English infantry.

In March, 1811, Masséna was removed from his
command. He crept miserably away, to bury his
shame in the retirement of the Marseilles command.
From that time forward his one aim was to enjoy
his riches in comfort; he made submission to the

Bourbons, and then reverted to Napoleon in 1815; after Waterloo he went back to the Bourbons.

But though he retained his wealth and his rank, there was yet further trouble awaiting him. His treason in 1815 had not been sufficiently extensive in that age of treason for him to suffer any penalty, and Louis XVIII., like the most humane Mikado, determined to make the punishment fit the crime as far as possible by appointing him one of Ney's judges. Masséna must have had a guilty conscience, and the horror of having to condemn his former colleague for the same crime as his own weighed heavily on him. At the same time the atrocious murder of his friend and fellow Marshal Brune during the White Terror at Avignon was a further blow. Tortured by remorse, hated by all parties alike, worn out with a life lived at high pressure, Masséna died in 1817 at the age of fifty-nine.

Masséna and Davout were the two foremost officers of Napoleon; the great contrast between them is due to the fact that one of them was guided by a strict sense of duty, the other merely by avarice.

There was another Marshal who is frequently considered to be at least the equal of these two, and the fact that he is so considered is peculiarly illustrative of his whole career, for Soult was for ever thrusting himself into the limelight and being elbowed out of it. Like many of the other Marshals, he rose from the ranks of the old regular army, and he first attained high rank by attracting Masséna's attention. He was second-in-command to that Marshal during the siege of Genoa, until he was taken prisoner during a sortie. He received his Marshalate in 1804, at a time when he was commanding a corps of the army at Boulogne, and he continued in command during the historic march to the Danube. At Austerlitz he was in command of the centre, and all his life he

considered that the battle was won mainly by himself.
He ignored Davout's splendid defence of the lake
defiles, Murat's wonderful handling of the cavalry
reserve, Lannes' management of the left, and Bernadotte's assault of the centre; he, and he alone, he
said, was responsible for Austerlitz.   He was greatly
disappointed when he was created Duke of Dalmatia
in 1808; he claimed that the only fitting title for
him was Duke of Austerlitz.   Napoleon ignored his
pleadings.

Soult fought at Jena, Eylau and Friedland, 1806-
1807, and was then sent to Spain.   To him was
entrusted the pursuit of Sir John Moore to Corunna,
and it cannot be denied that he failed in his mission.
Moore was never seriously engaged throughout the
retreat, and when finally Soult caught him up at
Corunna he was easily beaten back, despite his
superior numbers.   But for all that Soult had the
impertinence to claim a victory.

To him next was assigned the conquest of
Portugal; all he conquered was the northern
extremity; he was two months late in his arrival at
Oporto, and once there he settled down and would
not budge.   The reason for this delay soon emerged.
Soult was scheming for the crown of Portugal.   But
the plan evaporated promptly when Wellington
unexpectedly passed the Douro, surprised Soult in
his cantonments and bundled him out of Portugal,
compelling him to abandon his guns, his train, his
treasure, his sick—everything, in fact, except what
was on his men's backs.

Had Wellington ever suffered a similar reverse he
would probably have received the same treatment as
did Admiral Byng fifty years before, but Napoleon
was lenient and retained Soult in command.   The
new task assigned to him was the conquest of
Andalusia, and against the wretched Spanish armies
he achieved some remarkable successes.   Seville and

Granada fell before him; and he quietly proceeded to establish himself firmly and make his fortune. He looted cathedrals and treasuries, and sent the proceeds home. He ignored the Government of Madrid, and conducted himself like an independent and absolute monarch. Cadiz defied him, and all the efforts of his subordinate, Victor, Duke of Belluno, could not gain the place for him.

Masséna, held up at Torres Vedras by Wellington, with his army starving and disorganized, appealed to Soult for help. It was grudgingly given—too late. By the time Soult was ready to move upon the Tagus Masséna had already fallen back, utterly ruined. Soult was eventually stirred to action by Beresford's siege of Badajoz, but he met with an unexpected reverse at Albuera (which, characteristically, he claimed as a victory), and after that he was content to hold on to Andalusia until at last Wellington's victory at Salamanca and capture of Madrid compelled him to abandon his conquests. So exasperated was Joseph Bonaparte, King of Spain, by Soult's independence that he demanded Soult's recall, threatening abdication in the event of refusal. Napoleon complied, and during the beginning of 1813 Soult commanded the Guard in Germany, but after Vittoria he was sent back to try and keep the English out of France.

It was during this campaign of the Pyrenees that Soult's talents were exhibited at their best, but even here he failed. His manoeuvres, concentrations and determined counter-attacks are models of technical skill, but the fire, resolution and insight of greater generals are sadly lacking. He certainly delayed Wellington, and achieved a fair success considering the means at his disposal, but he was beaten back across the Pyrenees, back from Bayonne, from Orthez, and at last from Toulouse. Napoleon's abdication found Soult's army rapidly disintegrating,

and it is certain that the Duke of Dalmatia could
not have continued the struggle much longer.

In 1814 and 1815 Soult conducted himself as
might have been expected of a self-seeker.   He submitted to the Bourbons, but went over to Napoleon
as soon as the Emperor was on the throne after the
descent from Elba.

Napoleon appointed him chief of staff during the
Waterloo campaign.   The choice was unfortunate in
the event, but it is difficult to see what other course
the Emperor could have pursued.   Of the five
Marshals fit for service of whom Napoleon could
dispose, Davout had to be left to hold down Paris,
and Suchet had to guard the south.   Ney was
obviously useless for staff work, and Grouchy had
neither the brains nor the prestige for a position of
such vital responsibility.   So Soult took charge of
the staff, and the staff work was badly done.
Blunders were committed even in the orders given
for the crossing of the Sambre, and subsequently
delay followed delay and error followed error in fatal
sequence.   Ney, d'Erlon and Grouchy were in turn
misled by ambiguous orders.   The responsibility for
the failure of Waterloo is undoubtedly partly Soult's.

Naturally enough, Soult was proscribed after the
second Restoration, but after four years' exile, he
managed to ingratiate himself with the Bourbons,
and climbed steadily back to power by the aid of
hypocrisy and tuft-hunting.   The July revolution
brought him further power, and he was one of the
main props of Louis Philippe's authority.   In fact
the citizen king thought so much of him that he
made Soult Marshal-General of France, thus placing
him on a level with Saxe and Turenne.   He lived to
the venerable age of eighty-one, and died at last rich
and honoured above all the other soldiers of France.
His reputation grew steadily after the wars were over,
partly on account of Napier's liking for him, partly

on account of the natural tendency displayed by the
English to over-value a beaten antagonist, and partly
on account of his own deft powers of self-advertise-
ment.   His career is a striking example of the success
of cold, self-contained mediocrity.

There is only one other Marshal of Napoleon for
whom any claims to greatness have been made, and
that is Suchet, Duke of Albufera.   One of the most
interesting points about his career is that he had no
military training whatever before the Revolution.
As a young man of twenty-three years of age he
enlisted; at twenty-five he was a colonel.   He made
friends with the young Bonaparte at the siege of
Toulon, and later fought in the Italian campaign of
1796, gaining command of a brigade in 1797.

With the rank of general of division he served
Masséna and Joubert, and while Masséna held Genoa
in 1800 Suchet guarded the frontiers of France itself
on the Var.

But for eight years longer Suchet had to be content with the rank of a mere divisional commander,
leading a division of Lannes' corps at Austerlitz,
Jena and Friedland.   At last the wholesale toppling
of reputations in the Spanish war brought him his
chance, and he received command of the army of
Aragon.   To say the least, at first his position was
rather awkward.   His army was composed of raw
troops, shaken by the horrors of the siege of Saragossa; the Spaniards were in arms against him on all
sides; he was compelled by the neglect of the Paris
Government to live on the country; while to crown
it all he was expected to obey not only the orders
from Paris but also the frequently contradictory ones
from Joseph at Madrid.

We must give Suchet credit for coming through
the ordeal exceedingly well.   After an " unfortunate
incident " at Alcaniz, Suchet got his men well in
hand, and, by victories at Maria and Belchite, he

cleared Aragon of the enemy and proceeded to subdue
Catalonia. His way was barred in every direction by
fortresses, but, thanks partly to the folly of the
Spaniards and partly to his own resolution and
determination, he conquered the country inch by
inch. Somewhat cynically, in his memoirs, he tells
us that at the storming of Lerida he took care to drive
as many women and children as possible into the
citadel, and then by a vigorous bombardment he so
daunted the garrison that they surrendered. To
what total the casualties among the women and
children amounted before the surrender he does
not say.

Catalonia in his power, Suchet moved on to the
reduction of Valencia. His previous campaigns
repeated themselves. Battle followed siege, and
siege followed battle, until at last Suchet ruled all
Aragon, Catalonia and Valencia. Soult had already
conquered Andalusia, so that all Spain might, by
straining the truth a little, be said to be in the hands
of the French. For his achievements Suchet received
a Marshal's bâton, the title of Duke of Albufera and
half a million francs.

However, he was not fated to retain his conquests
long. Wellington's victory at Vittoria in 1813
brought about Suchet's evacuation of Valencia, just
as Salamanca had caused Soult to abandon Andalusia.

The same year an Anglo-Sicilian expedition under
Murray landed in Catalonia, and once more set aflame
the embers of the guerilla warfare. Suchet himself,
in action against unwontedly disciplined enemies,
met with a serious reverse at Castalla, but Murray
was too much of a nincompoop to follow up his
success. In the end Murray once more took ship,
and Suchet still held Catalonia and most of Aragon.
At this time he had a great opportunity to turn
against Wellington, who had his hands full with
Soult's offensive in the Pyrenees, but he let the

chance go. Immediately afterwards Lord William Bentinck, who had succeeded to Sir John Murray, kept him busy until the fall of the Empire. Soult's and Napoleon's demands had deprived Suchet of his best troops, and he did all that could be expected of him with the few men left to him.

In 1814 Suchet submitted to the Bourbons; in 1815 he betrayed them. During the Hundred Days he was ordered to secure the south-east with a few thousand men, and though unsuccessful, he accomplished much. After the Restoration the Bourbons refused to re-employ him.

Napoleon is credited with saying that Suchet was the best of his Marshals after Masséna's decay, and also that with two men like Suchet he would have held Spain against all endeavours. If Napoleon really did say this (and O'Meara's testimony is untrustworthy) Napoleon was wrong. The only time Suchet encountered English troops he was beaten; he was just as selfish and self-seeking as the other Marshals in Spain; he refused help whenever he could; and his success was due in a great part to the blunders of his opponents. Every French general and Marshal (Dupont excepted) succeeded against Spaniards; it was only against the English that they failed. Napoleon might just as well have said that Bessières was his best Marshal, because Bessières beat the Spaniards at Rio Seco while Masséna failed at Torres Vedras.

The one Marshal of Napoleon's whose career is more interesting in its pre-Revolutionary stages than under Napoleon is Augereau, Duke of Castiglione. He was a gigantic, swaggering fellow with a nose rendered brilliant by alcohol, devil-may-care and reckless, the ideal soldier of fortune. For he was a soldier of fortune. As a young man in the army of Louis XVI. he had killed one of his own officers on parade, and fled from the country with the police at

his heels.   In exile, he wandered through the East,
joined the Russian army, took part in the storming
of Ismail under Suvaroff, and then deserted.   Next
he joined the Prussian army, and served in the
Prussian Guard, but once more he deserted.   Desertion from the Prussian army was a difficult matter,
but Augereau achieved it by banding together all the
malcontents and fighting his way to the frontier.

On the birth of the Dauphin (later the unhappy
Louis XVII.) an amnesty was proclaimed in France,
and Augereau took advantage of it to rejoin his old
regiment, but once more tired of continuous service
and got himself sent off to Naples as an instructor
to the Neapolitan troops.   From Naples he eloped
with a Greek heiress to Lisbon, and in Lisbon he
annoyed the Inquisition, so that he was put in prison.

But still his luck held.   He escaped from the
clutches of the Holy Office, and arrived with his wife
in France just after the execution of Louis XVI.
His varied military experience naturally obtained him
high command in the Republican army; he fought in
La Vendée and in the Pyrenees, and then found
himself a divisional general under Napoleon in 1796.
In this campaign his reckless courage won him fame;
he was one of the heroes of the bridge of Lodi, and
at Castiglione it was his dashing leadership which
gained the day.

Augereau received the command of the army of
the Rhine after Bonaparte's departure for Egypt,
but, suspected of intriguing for the supreme power,
he was dismissed from his command, and, two years
later, he saw the prize fall into Napoleon's hands.
Napoleon bought Augereau's support with huge gifts
of money and, in 1804, a Marshal's bâton.

During the Austerlitz campaign Augereau was
only entrusted with the minor operation of subduing
Tyrol, but he fought well at Jena in 1806.   At Eylau
came disaster.   His corps, sent forward against the

AUGEREAU
DUC DE CASTIGLIONE

Russians in the teeth of a blinding snowstorm, lost direction, and was torn to pieces by a furious cannonade. Three-quarters of his men died; he himself, already gravely ill, was badly wounded.

Napoleon was furious. Augereau was sent home in disgrace, and what remained of the 7th Corps was broken up and distributed round the rest of the army. This was practically the end of Augereau's military life; he held command for a brief space during the war in Spain, but he failed again at Gerona and was superseded. By now he was well over fifty years of age, and dissipation had sapped his vitality. In 1814 and 1815 Augereau received commands of minor importance, his chief duty being the training of recruits, but his heart was not in his work. He lived long enough to betray Napoleon twice and the Bourbons once, and then died in 1816.

These brief biographies are sufficient to illustrate what kind of men the Marshals and their master were. With only a few exceptions they were all traitors, from Napoleon, plotting against the constitution he had sworn to uphold, to Ney, deserting his King. They were greedy, they were unscrupulous, they were selfish. Many of them were men of second-rate talent. Two attributes they had in common— extreme personal bravery and enormous experience in war. Soult is the only Marshal about whom we find any hints of cowardice (and there seems to be no foundation for these hints), while Suchet, Mortier and Brune were the only ones who had not served in the pre-Revolutionary army. None of the Marshals was a heaven-sent genius, and only one, Davout, combined loyalty and honesty with both military and administrative ability.

There is, of course, another side to the picture. If treachery can be excused at all, then there were good excuses for the treachery of every one of the guilty ones; if their talents appear mediocre to us now, it cannot be denied that they were nevertheless highly successful for a long period; if they were self-seeking, they were always ready, despite their riches and titles, to risk their lives in action at the head of their men.

The extravagant praise often meted out collectively to Napoleon's subordinates is undeserved, but somehow one can hardly avoid coming to the conclusion that a nation might well consider itself fortunate could it muster a similar array of men in high places.

CHAPTER X

BROTHERS

NAPOLEON was one of a large family, children of a shiftless father and a wonderful mother. Much the same might be said of a large number of other successful men—Moltke and Lincoln, for instance. But it is doubtful whether any importance from a eugenic point of view can be attached to this circumstance, for although some of the other Bonapartes showed undoubted talent in various directions, not one of them has ever displayed greatness comparable to the Emperor's. Biologically, Napoleon might be said to be a " sport," a " mutation," as de Vries would say. Yet even this theory is open to controversy, for mutations usually breed true, and none of Napoleon's children ever showed, as far as can be ascertained, any really striking amount of talent. Napoleon may thus be considered to be an isolated incident in his family history, one of the many immovable facts which are so gingerly skirted round by eugenists and other theorists.

What achievements can be ascribed to the brothers of the man who achieved so much? A few impracticable suggestions, a few novels (diluted St. Pierre, most of them), a few lost battles, a few lost kingdoms; beyond that—nothing. Louis was the father of Napoleon III., a clever man with many natural disadvantages mingled with his advantages. Lucien saved one unpleasant situation when president of the Council of Five Hundred in 1799. Jerome's grandson was a fairly eminent lawyer of the United States. The other Bonapartes were like their fathers and grandfathers before them, dilettanti, wobblers, unstable and irresponsible.

But useless as were Napoleon's brothers to him, he nevertheless bore with them patiently for years. A clannish clinging together is to be noticed in all their dealings, both while they were obscure and while they were powerful. An early Corsican environment may perhaps account for this, or perhaps it is to be ascribed to the intense pride in himself which Napoleon felt, and which perhaps was extended to all of his own blood.

Napoleon, the second son, and Joseph, the eldest, were separated from the other brothers and sisters by a gap of some seven years; the intervening children had died in infancy. When Charles Bonaparte, the father, died, therefore, it was upon these two that the headship of the family and the attendant responsibility fell. Joseph had already shown signs of his general uselessness. His mathematics and education generally had been too weak for him to have much chance of success in the army; he flinched from the Church, and therefore returned to Corsica to farm the few acres the Bonapartes possessed, and to carry on somehow, Micawber-like, until something turned up.

Napoleon, just appointed second-lieutenant of artillery, took upon himself to keep and educate the next brother, Louis. Since he had only thirty pounds a year pay, the struggle must have been terribly hard. After a year or two came the temporary success of the Paolists in Corsica, and as the Bonapartes had taken the French side the family had to fly to France for safety, leaving all

their property behind. Difficulties increased without number. The French Government, in the
throes of the Terror, had voted monetary support
for the refugees, but in the excitement of the
Toulon rebellion the decree was forgotten, and not
a sou was paid. St. Cyr, the State school for girls,
was closed, and another mouth, that of the eldest
daughter, Elise, had to be fed by the struggling
family.

But then everything suddenly changed for the
better. Napoleon, after distinguishing himself at
Toulon, fought his way up to the rank of chef de
brigade. Joseph obtained a commissaryship in the
army of Italy through the aid of a fellow Corsican,
Salicetti. Then also he married Mademoiselle Clary,
daughter of a Marseilles merchant. Her dowry
must have appeared enormous to the famished
Bonapartes—it amounted to no less than six
thousand pounds sterling. None of the Bonapartes
could as yet foresee the day when any one of them
would spend six thousand pounds on their most
trifling whim.

A year later Napoleon saved the Directory from
the revolt of the sections, and the family was at last
in comparatively smooth water. With Napoleon in
command of the Army of the Interior, influence
could be brought to bear to help his brothers.
Louis became his aide-de-camp. Lucien received a
commissaryship with the Army of the North, while
immediately afterwards the horizon of possibilities
was widened still further by Napoleon's appointment to the command in Italy and his amazing
victories there. Joseph received important diplomatic appointments at Parma and Rome. Louis
distinguished himself with the army. Lucien at
this time was the black sheep of the family. He
threw up one appointment after another; he
expressed undesirable opinions with undesirable

G

force, and finally he married a completely illiterate girl of the Midi. However, Napoleon forgave him, and before setting out for Egypt he enabled him to secure election to the Council of Five Hundred. Lucien had always been, even in Corsica, a ranting rhetorician, and in the Council he would be able to indulge his bent to his heart's desire. Jerome, the youngest brother, was still at school, and he had to master as best he could his disappointment at not accompanying Napoleon to Egypt. Eugène Beauharnais, his schoolfellow, was going; he asked bitterly why he could not go also, leaving out of calculation the years of difference in their ages.

Napoleon returned from Egypt to find his brothers had somewhat improved their positions. Lucien was president of the Council of Five Hundred; Joseph's diplomatic services had enabled him to enter intimately into the Directory circles, so that Napoleon was at once able to plunge into the welter of politics. The *coup d'état* of the 19th Brumaire was planned. Joseph acted as intermediary between Napoleon, Sièyes, Ducos, Bernadotte (now his brother-in-law), Fouché and Moreau. Lucien made himself responsible for the Council, and arranged for the vital meeting to be held at Versailles. Their united efforts gained for Napoleon the command of the Army of the Interior. Everything was in readiness. On the morning of the 19th the Upper House, the Council of Ancients, readily bowed to the will of the great soldier, but the Council of Five Hundred were not so willing to pronounce their own sentence of extinction.

Murmurs arose and grew louder, and when Napoleon appeared before them he was greeted with fierce cries. Half of the Five Hundred were old *sans-culottes*, men who had gambled with their lives for power under Hébert and Danton, and when Napoleon, for the only time in his career, flinched from danger, the dreadful cry which had announced Robespierre's fall arose. "Hors la loi! Hors la loi!" shouted the deputies. Napoleon staggered out of the council hall, apparently ruined.

Lucien Bonaparte leaped into the breach. He spoke fervently on behalf of his brother, but he was shouted down by the furious deputies. Somebody demanded a motion of outlawry against Napoleon; Lucien refused to put it to the vote. Neither side would give way, and the passions grew fiercer and fiercer. Suddenly Lucien tore off the insignia of his office, and even as he did so the door flew open and Napoleon's troops burst in. Leclerc, Napoleon's brother-in-law, was at their head. "The Council is dissolved," said Leclerc, and the soldiers cleared the hall with fixed bayonets. Napoleon had utilized to the full the few minutes Lucien had gained for him. He had inflamed the soldiers with tales of treachery and assassination. On the evening of the same day a rump of the Council met under Lucien's presidency and confirmed Napoleon in all the powers he demanded.

At first sight this action of Lucien's appears invaluable. Nevertheless, on further consideration one realizes that Napoleon could have succeeded without it. When Bernadotte was King of Sweden, he told the French Ambassador, apropos of some news regarding French parliamentary criticism, that if he were King of France with two hundred thousand soldiers at his back he would put his tongue out at the chamber of deputies. Napoleon at the time of the *coup d'état*, had not merely two hundred thousand soldiers, but the whole weight of public opinion at his back. No decree of outlawry by a discredited Council of Five Hundred could injure him.

For all this, Lucien was of great use to Napoleon during the Consulate. As Tribune, he employed his undoubted parliamentary gifts to foist on the legislative various unpalatable measures. He skilfully defended the proposed Legion of Honour to an acutely suspicious House, and then finally he effected a judicious weeding of the Senate and Corps Législatif during the retirements of 1802. For all these services he was made Grand Officer of the Legion of Honour, and a Senator; he received a large official income and a palace (Poppesdorf on the Moselle), while it seemed as if it would not be long before he received royal honours. Napoleon proposed that he should act as French agent in the Kingdom of Etruria; the Queen was recently widowed; a marriage would follow naturally, and Lucien would be proclaimed king. As far as Napoleon knew, there was no legal bar to such an arrangement, for Lucien's illiterate wife had died some time back, but the proposal forced Lucien to make an announcement he should have made earlier. In 1803 he had secretly married a widow, Madame Jouberthon, who had been his mistress for a year, and actually had borne him a child the day before the ceremony.

This was the end of things as far as Lucien was concerned. Napoleon quarrelled violently with him, and Lucien left the country. He lived for a time in Rome, where Pius VII. made him Prince of Canino, but had to move on at the French occupation. He tried to reach the United States, but the English prevented this, as they feared he might have designs on Spanish America. They could have known little about the dilatory, hesitating æsthete to imagine he was capable of any action of importance. Lucien was brought a prisoner to England, and he promptly settled down and made himself comfortable at Ludlow, perfectly contented to enjoy his books, his scientific dabblings, his pictures, in peace. Once only did he rouse himself, and that was during the

Hundred Days. The old clan feeling apparently re-awoke, and he was at Napoleon's side during that brief period. But as soon as Napoleon had left for St. Helena, and three months in a Piedmontese prison had cooled his own blood, he went back to Rome and continued his placid existence until his death in 1840. Two or three feeble novels and one frigid epic stand to his credit—further comment appears unnecessary; if a man with Lucien's opportunities abandons them in favour of a mild life of artistic enjoyment, he must be either a great man or a very small man, and Lucien was not a great man.

But Lucien had at any rate the hardihood to stand up to his terrible brother about his marriage; Louis and Jerome gave way in a ridiculous fashion.

Louis allowed himself to be persuaded into marrying Hortense Beauharnais, Napoleon's step-daughter, thereby making his sister-in-law Josephine into his mother-in-law as well. No love was lost between the newly-married pair, and they drifted apart after a month or two of married life. A child, Napoleon Charles, was born at the end of 1802, and Napoleon was popularly credited with being its incestuous father. At first he did his utmost to check these rumours, but later he tried to use them for his own ends—a scheme nipped in the bud by the child's death from croup in 1807. Napoleon repeatedly tried to reconcile the parents, and on two occasions he met with success. The product of the first reconciliation was a child, Napoleon Louis, born in 1804, who died during the Carbonari insurrection in Italy in 1831, and the product of the second reconciliation was another child who later became Napoleon III.

On Louis, for his compliance, honours and wealth were heaped in profusion. He became a Prince of the Empire, with a million francs a year; as Constable of France, and consequently a Grand

Imperial Dignitary, he received one third of a million francs a year; he was Governor of Paris; a member of the Council of State; in precedence only the Emperor and Joseph Bonaparte came before him. Louis found himself the third person in the Empire with an annual income of about eighty thousand pounds sterling.

Yet even this was not all. Austerlitz had laid Europe at Napoleon's feet, and he used his power to the full. The rulers of Bavaria and Würtemberg became kings; a terse proclamation announced that the Bourbon house of Naples had "ceased to reign," and Masséna with sixty thousand men swept into the country to establish Joseph Bonaparte on the throne. Louis was given the kingdom of Holland. Just before, Napoleon had offered the crown of Italy to these two brothers in turn, but they had refused it, partly on account of the utter dependence of Italy upon France, and partly because one condition of acceptance was resignation of all claims upon the throne of France.

Holland, when Louis arrived, was in a bad way. Her people were ground down by remorseless taxation; the Continental system was ruining them rapidly; the conscription was exhausting them; and the outlook generally was hopeless. In fact they were so sunk in despondency that on one occasion, when Napoleon called a plebiscite among them to decide on their Government, only one-sixth of the voters troubled to vote. With the advent of Louis they hoped for better things, but Louis was the kind of man from whom it is better to hope for nothing. His health was bad, his domestic troubles upset him, his terrible brother held him completely under his thumb, and tumbled over like card houses all his tentative schemes of improvement. Matters in Holland went from bad to worse. At intervals the wretched Louis roused himself, and tried to help his subjects, but every time the thunders of Napoleon daunted him.

At last, in 1810, he found the French demanding military occupation of Holland as the only way to secure the thorough observance of the Continental system. A French division was marching on Amsterdam, and fighting was threatened between the Dutch troops and the French. Louis dropped his kingly dignity as if it were red-hot; he abdicated in favour of his son, Napoleon Louis, and then, leaving his wife and family behind, he fled across the frontier and never stopped until he was safe in Austria. Neither threats nor cajoleries on Napoleon's part were able to bring him back to France and the undignified dignities which were offered him. He settled down with relief in Styria with his books and his artistic studies. A novel or two and some peculiarly unsatisfying memoirs were all he left behind after his death.

Hortense, his wife, found means to console herself. The Comte de Flahault became a frequent visitor at her house in Paris, and a son was eventually born to her, who became, under the Second Empire, the Duc de Morny. Flahault himself was with good reason believed to be a son of the great Talleyrand, Prince of Benevento, so that de Morny had the proud privilege of calling himself a doubly illegitimate grandson of Talleyrand, an illegitimate Beauharnais, an illegitimate Flahault and a natural brother of Napoleon III. A highly satisfactory pedigree, in truth.

It appeared at first as though Joseph Bonaparte would have better fortune than Lucien or Louis. He had already held positions of great responsibility as Ambassador and Plenipotentiary, and in 1806 he became King of Naples. His rule at first was precarious, for although many of the Neapolitans acquiesced in his elevation, the English, and the

Bourbons who still held Sicily did their best to make him as uncomfortable as possible. By landing banditti, galley-slaves and unpleasant characters generally, they kept Calabria in a blaze. A small English force was landed, won a battle at Maida, and then had to retire. But with fifty thousand Frenchmen at his back Joseph gradually wore down opposition and established himself more or less firmly.

However, this had hardly been accomplished when in 1808 he was suddenly called back to France and proclaimed King of Spain and the Indies. As regards the Indies, Joseph was divided from them by the British fleet, and if the fleet could preserve Sicily for the Italian Bourbons, it could most certainly preserve America for the Spanish ones. The Atlantic is a good deal wider than the Straits of Messina. As regards Spain the position was only not quite so difficult. The whole country was in rebellion, it is true; three weeks before the streets of Madrid had run knee-deep with the blood of Spaniards and Frenchmen. Some thirty thousand of his subjects had to be beaten in a pitched battle before Joseph could enter his capital, but Napoleon promised him two hundred thousand French soldiers to support him, and Joseph, a little bewildered, a little timorous, proceeded with the adventure. He reached Madrid, and sent his armies forward to subdue his kingdom. In three weeks one army, under Moncey, had been beaten back from Valencia with ruinous losses, while twenty thousand men under Dupont were hemmed in at Baylen and compelled to surrender. A hundred thousand Spaniards were marching on Madrid, and the King of Spain returned with all speed to the security of the French armies on the Ebro. Another battle had to be fought before this sanctuary could be gained. Immediately afterwards came the news that the pestilent English, for ever intruding themselves

JOSEPH NAPOLÉON ROI DE NAPLES et de SICILE
ET ROI D'ESPAGNE ET DES INDES
Né le 7 Janvier 1768 Sacre et couronné le
30 Mars 1806.

uninvited, had landed in Portugal, beaten Junot
and cleared Portugal of the French by the
Convention of Cintra. Napoleon at this moment
was at the Conference of Erfürt, trying to dis-
entangle the politics of Russia, Austria, Prussia and
the Rhenish Confederation, but as soon as he could
he ended this meeting, issued a few hasty orders to
organize his army against a probable attack by
Austria in the spring, and rushed back across
Europe bent upon settling the affair out of hand.
Calling up eighty thousand more troops, he pushed
suddenly over the Ebro. The Spanish armies were
shattered in three battles at Gamonal, Espinosa
and Tudela. Once more Joseph was established in
Madrid, but the English again interfered. A skilful
thrust by Sir John Moore against the French communications led to the French armies being wheeled
against him instead of pushing on to complete the
overthrow of the Spaniards. In the middle of this
movement Napoleon was called back to Paris on
account of the Austrian trouble and the plottings
of Talleyrand and Fouché; Joseph was left in
Madrid, King of a country ablaze with rebellion,
and commander of an army openly contemptuous.

Joseph bore his troubles for five years. Madrid
and its environs were just able to bear the expense
of his guard and his court; the rest of the country
was parcelled out among French generals who ruled
their districts despotically as far as the English and
the partidas would allow them. Joseph simply did
not count; his pathetic appeals to his protectors to
combine as he wished were disregarded. Time and
again he asked Napoleon either to give him full
power or to relieve him of the burden of his mock
sovereignty, but Napoleon bullied him into continuing with the farce. In 1812 he lost Madrid for
a time, and in 1813 he lost all Spain. He gathered
together all his possessions, and tried to retire in

as dignified a fashion as possible. Forced by
Wellington to fight at Vittoria, he was badly
beaten and driven off his line of communications.
Everything had to be abandoned. During the
flight Joseph left his carriage by one door while
the English Hussars entered it by the other, pistol
shots were fired at him, and altogether he was hardly
treated with the dignity a King deserves. All his
court paraphernalia was captured by the English.
His carriage was found stuffed with masterpieces;
he lost gold to the value of a million sterling, and his
plate, his personal belongings, and his lady friends
were alike left behind. Soult at last arrived to
hold the line of the Pyrenees, and Joseph was
ignominiously thrust aside.

He pathetically re-entered the limelight in Paris
during the fatal early months of 1814, but he was no
longer taken seriously. A proclamation of his to the
people of Paris, practically telling them to have no
fear for he was with them was received with howls
of derision. He pottered helplessly about until the
abdication, he figured inconspicuously in the last
gathering of the Bonaparte clan during the Hundred
Days, and then went off to America. He shook
from his shoulders with relief the burden of king-
ship. As with his brothers, feeble novels and the
study of literature engaged his attention from 1815
until his death.

A third brother of Napoleon's was also a king;
he also was thrust on to an unwilling people, and he
also was thrust off again in course of time. Jerome
was the hope of the family; in 1801, at the age of
seventeen, he appeared to give promise of great gifts.
Napoleon sent him off to join the navy and to
acquire manhood in that hardest of all schools.
The First Consul's plan was defeated, for the
officers of the squadron hastened to make the great
man's young brother as comfortable as possible.

When Gantheaume, with vastly superior numbers, fell in with and captured the English *Swiftsure*, Jerome (seventeen years old, if you please) was sent to receive the English captain's sword. On the West Indian station the French admiral bluntly told Jerome that he was bound to become an admiral anyway, and he should work hard, not to achieve promotion but to be ready for it. Jerome did not follow his advice. The renewal of war with England in 1803 found Jerome still in the West Indies, and he left his ship (which was subsequently captured) and went off to the United States. At Washington he found the French Ambassador, Pichon, and drew lavishly on him for funds and embarrassed the worthy man enormously. Jerome had quite a nice little holiday in America, travelling about from place to place, making hordes of friends, spending thousands of dollars, and being generally lionized.

The climax was reached when at the age of nineteen he informed the wretched Pichon that he had just married a Miss Elizabeth Patterson, daughter of a worthy Baltimore merchant, and asked him for further funds to support his new condition. Pichon was horrified. The marriage was illegal by the law of France, it is true, but Jerome apparently took it seriously. Napoleon would be mad with rage. Pichon saw himself deprived of his position and driven into exile. He implored Jerome to go home. Jerome refused. Pichon cut off supplies. Jerome gaily borrowed from his new father-in-law. Then came the news that Napoleon had proclaimed himself Emperor of the French. Madame Jerome Bonaparte naturally wanted to go to France as soon as possible and enjoy her rank as an Imperial Princess. Jerome had doubts on the subject, but at last, when his funds ran low, he set out in one of Mr. Patterson's ships for Lisbon with his wife. At Lisbon what Jerome had feared came about. The French consul, acting on instructions from Paris, announced that he could give only Jerome a passport; he could not give " Miss Patterson " one. At first Jerome swore he would stay by his wife, but Napoleon's emissaries made him tempting offers. If he abandoned Miss Patterson he would be made an Imperial Prince; he would have high command; he would receive at least 150,000 francs a year. Jerome succumbed. He told his wife to travel round by sea to Amsterdam, whence she could more easily reach Paris to join him. He himself went direct. Naturally by Napoleon's orders Elizabeth was denied permission to land at Amsterdam; she at last realized what Jerome had done, and, as she could do nothing else, she went to England, where she was cordially received. A child was born to her while she was in lodgings at Camberwell, and this son's son was in 1906 Attorney-General of the United States. But Elizabeth was never recognized by the French Government as Jerome's wife, and eventually she went back to the United States. There is a story that many years after she encountered Jerome and his next wife, Catherine of Würtemberg, in a picture gallery at Florence. Jerome was a perfect gentleman, and passed her by after telling Catherine who she was.

Be that as it may, Jerome gained many solid advantages from his desertion of his wife. His debts were paid and a large income was allowed him. He was entrusted with the command of a small naval expedition against Algiers, and on his return to Genoa with a few score French prisoners whom he had released he was greeted with storms of salutes and congratulatory addresses. From the tone of the announcements one would gather that he had anticipated Lord Exmouth's feat in 1816, bombarded the city and wrung submission from the

Dey by daring and courage. As a matter of fact the prisoners had been ransomed before he even started for a few pounds each by a French representative sent specially over.

It was much the same with the West Indian expedition which followed. Jerome certainly did considerable damage to English commerce, and somehow escaped the English cruisers, but the official description of his exploits seemed to indicate that he had almost subverted the British Empire.

No sooner was Jerome back in France than he turned soldier. On his early naval expeditions he had strutted about the deck in a Hussar uniform of which he was very fond, but apparently he did not see fit to appear before his troops in naval attire by way of returning the compliment. Napoleon was already planning to give Jerome a German kingdom, and he therefore decided that the young man should gain some military experience along with as much military glory as possible. With Vandamme as his adviser and a strong *corps d'armée* at his back, Jerome plunged into Silesia. The Prussians were stunned by the defeats of Jena and Auerstädt, and by the relentless pursuit which had followed, and they gave way before him with hardly a blow struck. One or two fortresses showed signs of resistance, and were blockaded. The remainder of the province was soon in Jerome's hands, and he and Vandamme and the divisional commanders promptly enriched themselves with plunder. Once more Jerome's achievements were blazoned abroad as feats of marvellous skill. Napoleon was usually successful in obtaining the gold of devotion in return for the tinsel of propaganda, and now he was exerting all his arts in his brother's favour.

Napoleon's victory of Friedland was followed by the Treaty of Tilsit, and one of the clauses therein gave Westphalia to Jerome. At the mature age of

twenty-three the young man found himself ruler of
two millions of subjects.   Moreover, he was given a
royal bride.   The King of Würtemberg, it is true,
had not been a king for more than two years, but
the house of Wittelsbach could trace its ancestry
back to the time of Charlemagne.   Catherine of
Würtemberg was already affianced, but at the
Emperor's command the engagement was broken
off and Catherine was given to Jerome.   Jerome's
American marriage was declared null and void, first
by Napoleon because at the time Jerome was a
minor, and secondly by the Metropolitan of Paris,
for no particular reason.   The fact that the ceremony
had been performed by a Roman Catholic archbishop
with all due regard to the forms of the Church, did
not count.

However, the splendours of the new marriage
were such that the old one might well be forgotten.
It took place in the gallery of Diana at the Tuileries,
and was attended by all the shining lights of the
Empire.   There was a goodly assembly of Kings,
and there were Princes and Grand Dukes in dozens.
Everybody seemed to have made a special effort to
wear as much jewellery as possible, and the display
of diamond-sewn dresses and yard-long ropes of
pearls was remembered for years afterwards.   The
Democratic Empire had certainly made great strides.

Once married, Jerome departed with his Queen
to his kingdom of Westphalia.   The new state was
a curious mixture of fragments of other countries.
Hesse, Hanover, Brunswick and Prussia had all con-
tributed to it (unwillingly), and Calvinists and
Catholics were represented in about equal numbers
and with an equal aversion each from the other.
The whole country was ruined by prolonged military
occupation; it was loaded with debt, for Napoleon
blithely began to collect money owing to the Elector
of Hesse whom he had dispossessed; nearly one-

fourth of the whole area was claimed by the Emperor to be distributed as endowments to his officers; a huge army had to be maintained, and a French army of occupation had to be paid and supplied; a war contribution had to be paid to the French treasury; and to crown it all the Continental system was slowly crushing the life out of the industries. During the first administrative year there was a deficit of five million francs, and this was the smallest there was during the whole lifetime of the country. From then onwards the financial measures proceeded on the well-worn way to ruin, the landmarks thereon being forced loans, repudiation of debt, and taxes amounting to one-half the total national income. There is nothing remarkable in the fact that the six years of the existence of the kingdom were marked by two serious mutinies and three distinct rebellions.

Jerome himself was quite indifferent to the troubles of his people. He spent enormous amounts on his palace at Cassel, and in addition he fell heavily into personal debt despite a Civil List of five million francs a year. His pleasures were, to say the least, of a dubious sort, and we find hints everywhere that the orgies at Cassel eclipsed even those at the Parc-aux-Cerfs in the good old days of the Bourbon régime. Catherine apparently made no violent objection to this behaviour of her husband's; the graceless young scamp seems to have completely bewitched her. He must have had the time of his life during these years, despite occasional shocks like the one he experienced when he read in the *Moniteur* (the first indication he received) that one quarter of his kingdom had been annexed to France.

Only once did Jerome appear on active service during this period, and that was to command thirty or forty thousand men during the Russian campaign of 1812. He travelled with all the luxuries he could think of, equerries, cooks, valets, barbers, mistresses,

until his headquarters appeared like a small town.
But the hardships of war did not last long; Jerome
was found wanting in military ability.   His failure
to keep up to the difficult time-table Napoleon set
him during the advance into Lithuania led to his
being placed under Davout's command.   Neither he
nor Davout liked the arrangement, and Jerome threw
up his command and went back to Cassel.

Here he enjoyed himself for one more year.
Even he had flinched from reviving the old *droit du
seigneur*, but he did his best in that direction without
that amount of ceremony.   But the sands were
running out as the French armies fell back from the
Niemen to the Oder, from the Oder to the Elbe, and
at last the battle of Leipzig laid open all the country
between the Elbe and the Rhine to the triumphant
Allies.   The Kingdom of Westphalia vanished in a
night, like a dream; the Westphalian army went over
to the Allies *en bloc*, and Jerome returned to France
with barely two hundred men at his back.

The Hundred Days gave Jerome one last chance
of displaying his manhood, and, curiously enough,
he made the most of it.   He was given command of
a division of Reille's corps in the Waterloo campaign,
and he led it with unexpected dash and vigour.   He
fought heroically at Quatre Bras, exposing himself
recklessly in the dreadful fighting in the wood.   At
Waterloo he headed the attack on Hougomont, leading assault after assault with unflinching bravery.   He
was wounded, but remained in action, and at the close
of the day he was seen striving to rally his men when
they broke panic-stricken before the allied advance.

Waterloo almost atones in the general estimation
for Jerome's long and useless life.   After the second
Restoration he drifted idly about Europe, accompanied by his devoted Catherine; when the Orleans
monarchy fell he hastened back to France.   Along
with Louis Napoleon he planned the *coup d'état*, and

for the rest of his life, until 1860, he was once more a prominent subject of the French Empire. Napoleon III. made him a Marshal; his son married a princess of the house of Savoy, and he died comfortably in bed at the age of seventy-six. He never met with any fatal retribution for his callous desertion of Elizabeth Patterson, or for the wild debauchery of his youth. There seems to be no moral to attach to the tale of his career.

Of the remaining descendants in the male line of the house of Bonaparte there is little to tell. One of them, Lucien, a grandson of Lucien, Napoleon's brother, rose to the eminence of Cardinal; one or two of them have shown ability in various branches of science; the curious tendency to literature has repeatedly cropped out; but none of them has ever achieved anything really striking. Their novels are more feeble even than Garibaldi's, while their political achievements are of course beneath comparison. Some of them have fought duels, and some of them have committed manslaughter. Some of them have even attained the dazzling heights of the French chamber of deputies. But there is not one of them who would receive two lines of notice in any fair-sized book of reference were it not for his relationship to the great Napoleon. The present head of the house is Napoleon Victor Jerome, who married in 1910 a Coburg princess, a member of the royal family of Belgium. He is Napoleon VI., if the principle of legitimacy can yet be applied to the house of Bonaparte; anyway, he shows not the least desire to become Napoleon VI.

Had Napoleon had no brothers, he would probably have been more successful; had he had any brothers of equal ability they would have pulled each other down in Europe, if they had not cut each other's throats years before in Corsica; as it is, he stands as unique in his family as he does in his age.

H

CHAPTER XI

SISTERS

IF Napoleon's brothers were all a generally hopeless lot, the same can by no means be said of his sisters. These stood out head and shoulders above the other women of the time; they were all distinguished by their force of character; whether they were married to nonentities or personalities they all did their best to wear the breeches—but they did not flinch from wearing nothing at all if the whim took them. They were all handsome women, and one of them, Pauline, was generally considered to be the most beautiful woman of the time.

Napoleon's sisters resembled him much more closely than did his brothers. Xerxes, watching Artemisia fighting desperately at Salamis, exclaimed, "This woman plays the man while my men play the woman," and a dispassionate observer of the conduct of the rulers of the countries of Europe in the Napoleonic era might well say the same. One has only to compare Joseph Bonaparte flying from Vittoria, or Murat flying from Tolentino, with Caroline rallying the Neapolitans, Louise of Prussia fighting desperately hard against fate at Tilsit, and Marie Caroline of Bourbon directing Sicily's struggle with the great conqueror.

There are obvious differences, too, between Napoleon's treatment of his brothers and his treatment of his sisters. Joseph and Jerome and Louis

114

he bullied unmercifully, but it was far otherwise with Pauline, Caroline and Elise. He himself admitted that he always " formed into line of battle " in preparation for an interview with Caroline, and although authorities are at variance as to when he actually said to his family that anyone would think he was trying to rob them of the inheritance of the late King, their father, it is certain that the remark was addressed to his sisters and mother. They were all of them women with a very keen sense of what they wanted, and they fought like tiger-cats to obtain it.

The three girls all married before or during the Consulate, when Napoleon had not yet attained the heights he reached later, so that the marriages they made were by no means as brilliant as they might have been, and fell far short of the marriages which Napoleon arranged for much more distant relatives who became marriageable at a later period. Elise was old enough to experience acutely the trials of poverty which overtook the family before Napoleon was promoted to important commands. She was sent as a child to school at St. Cyr, a state-supported institution under the patronage of the Bourbons, and had to leave there at the same time as the Bonaparte family had to fly from Corsica to Marseilles. During the next few years she was rather a trial to her family, for she flirted with every man she met, eligible and ineligible. One of her admirers was Admiral Truguet, who was a thoroughly good sailor and quite a good match at that time, but Madame Bonaparte declined to allow the affair to develop. In the end it was a fellow Corsican, Félix Baciocchi, who gained her hand. Baciocchi was a distant connection of the Bonaparte family, and also, by a curious coincidence, he was a relation of Charles Andrea Pozzo di Borgo, another Corsican, who is believed to have been at feud with the Bonapartes, and who certainly distinguished himself, while in the service of various

European monarchs, by his virulent hatred of Napoleon.

But Baciocchi did not distinguish himself at all. He was a complete nonentity, with neither the desire nor the capacity to achieve power. At the marriage Elise only brought him thirty thousand francs as dowry (her share of the Bonaparte property, now recovered from the Paolists), but after 1797 Napoleon was able to make Elise presents of considerably greater value. Baciocchi was then a major of infantry; but during the Consulate his wife endeavoured to obtain higher military command for him. So persistently did she scheme to this end that at last in self-defence Napoleon made him a senator in order to cut short his military career.

Pauline, the next sister, married Leclerc, a capable soldier, who rendered Napoleon valuable service during the *coup d'état* of Brumaire. He, at least, was worthy of promotion, and Bonaparte gave it to him lavishly. But it was Caroline, the youngest, who looked after herself best. Most of the generals of the Consulate sought her hand, including Lannes, but both Napoleon and Caroline desired alliance with the greatest of them all, Moreau. However, Moreau declined the honour (thereby directly bringing about his own exile soon after), and Caroline chose for herself a husband of whose military talents she was sufficiently sure to be certain that high command would be given him, but who also was sufficiently weak-willed to be well under her thumb. Lannes was of too lofty a type to please her in this respect, and his personal devotion to Napoleon was undoubted; Caroline therefore selected a young cavalry officer, Murat.

Pauline experienced an unfortunate beginning to the career she had planned for herself and her husband. Leclerc was appointed to the command of the expeditionary force which was sent to subdue

Hayti, and Pauline was ordered to accompany him.
In vain she pleaded ill-health; in vain she said that
her complexion would be ruined by the West Indian
sun; Napoleon was adamant. Pauline kept up the
plea of ill-health sufficiently well to be carried on
board ship at Brest in a litter, but the expedition
started. As was only to be expected, it ended in
disastrous failure. Toussaint l'Ouverture, the leader
of the rebellion, was indeed captured and sent to
France to perish in a freezing mountain prison, but
yellow fever attacked the French troops, and they
died in thousands. Leclerc was one of those who
perished.

Napoleon himself was able to gain some satisfaction even from the failure, because the men he had
sent had all been drawn from the Army of the Rhine,
and they were all guilty of the crime of believing that
Moreau was a great man, and that Hohenlinden was
a greater victory than Marengo. But, as has been
said, the French died in thousands; the negroes
fought stoutly, and at last after fifteen thousand
Frenchmen had perished only a miserable fragment
of the expeditionary force survived to be withdrawn
under Rochambeau. Pauline returned to France to
deplore her ruined complexion.

However, with the establishment of the Empire
the sisters found plenty to occupy their minds in
acquiring as much spoil as possible. Money they
sought greedily, and Napoleon gave them millions of
francs. They shed tears of rage when they found
that the Emperor expected them to remain content
with being plain Mesdames Murat, Leclerc and
Baciocchi, while the hated Josephine was Sa Majesté
Impériale et Royale l'Impératrice et Reine, and
while plain Julie Clary and Hortense Beauharnais
(Joseph's and Louis's wives) were Imperial and Royal
Highnesses. Napoleon gave way to their bitter
pleadings and at one stroke created them Princesses

of the Empire, making their husbands Princes at the
same time.

These names, Elise, Pauline and Caroline, were
not the baptismal names of the ladies concerned.   At
baptism they had been given Italian names, each of
them attached to the ever popular name of Maria.
Their mother was Maria Letizia; while Elise was
really Maria Anna, Pauline, Maria Paoletta and
Caroline, Maria Annunziata.   It is by these names
that they are described on their marriage certificates,
but they dropped them soon afterwards to assume
names which appealed to them more.   Changing
their names did not change their natures; they
intrigued and schemed and plotted; they flirted; they
sought favours; they quarrelled with their husbands,
with their sisters-in-law, and with each other; in fact
they exhibited all the fierce self-seeking which
characterized the ladies of the old monarchy.   There
was this difference, however.   Fifty years before the
Court ladies had intrigued for places, and for
thousands of francs.   Now they intrigued for
kingdoms and millions.

Caroline early took first place in the race for
power.   Her husband, Murat, distinguished himself
in the Austerlitz campaign by capturing the great
bridge over the Danube by a trick which savoured
rather of treachery, and by bold heading of cavalry
charges at Austerlitz itself.   He was already a Prince
and second senior Marshal of the Empire; the only
possible promotion left for him was a sovereignty.
Napoleon, carving out his Confederation of the
Rhine, found him one.   A tiny area on the Rhine
was obtained by exchange from Prussia and Bavaria,
and Murat and Caroline became Grand Duke and
Grand Duchess of Berg and Cleves.   Caroline was
in no way satisfied.   She egged her husband on to
demand increases of territory, privileges of toll on
the Rhine, and so on, until the little state had set

both France and Prussia in a ferment. The tension
hardly relaxed until, a month or two later, war broke
out between the two countries. Murat went away
with the Grand Army to Jena, Eylau and Friedland;
Caroline stayed behind in Paris to guard their
interests. She did it well. She indulged in an outrageous flirtation with Junot, Governor of Paris,
and hints have not been wanting that her purpose
was to arrange a revolution rather on the same lines
as Mallet tried to follow in 1812. At her palace of
the Elysée (now the official residence of the President
of the Third Republic) she gave the most brilliant
fêtes imaginable. She worked like a slave to gain
popularity, so that she could gain the throne in the
event of her brother's death. Then Tilsit followed
Friedland, and the Emperor returned. The
campaign had brought more glory to Murat than
he had as yet gained. He had headed the marvellous
pursuit after Jena, when he had captured fortresses
with a few regiments of Hussars, and it was largely
through him that practically the whole Prussian army
had fallen into the hands of the French. At Eylau,
when Augereau's corps had come reeling back
through the blizzard, shattered and almost annihil-
ated, when it seemed as though the Grand Army
was at last going to taste defeat, Napoleon had called
on Murat to save the day. Murat replied by charging at the head of eighteen thousand cavalry. He
broke up the first Russian line, captured thousands
of prisoners, and beat back the Russians until Davout
and Ney were in position.

Naturally, he reaped vast rewards. His Grand
Duchy was doubled in size; millions of francs were
bestowed upon him and upon Caroline; but they
were hugely dissatisfied. Murat had hoped for the
crown of Poland, or, failing that, for a whole
kingdom in Germany. But Poland was given to the
King of Saxony, and the creation of Jerome Bona-

parte's kingdom of Westphalia shut out all hopes of
the further expansion of Berg.   Caroline and Murat
were furious.   Murat showed his rage by hinting at
rebellion; Caroline used her native Corsican guile and
became as friendly to Napoleon as possible, helping
him in his affairs with women, recounting to him the
tittle-tattle of the drawing-rooms of Paris, and even
at times giving him the shelter of her roof to conceal
from Josephine some of his more flagrant unfaith-
fulnesses.

However, Murat was soon in employment again.
He was appointed to the command in Spain,
where Napoleon's tortuous intrigues to dispossess
the unspeakable Bourbons were beginning to take
effect.   Murat certainly achieved fair success.   He
gained possession of the Spanish fortresses, stamped
out the little spurts of rebellion which occasionally
flamed out, and by the time the outrageous treaty of
Bayonne had been signed he was in a position to
hand over to Napoleon the greater part of the
country.   Another disappointment awaited him.
He had hoped that all this mysterious business would
result in his being given the crown of Spain—but
Joseph Bonaparte received it instead, and Murat and
Caroline were forced to be content with Joseph's
former kingdom of Naples.   Caroline was at last a
Queen.

The royal pair began at once to treat their new
kingdom much as Sancho Panza had determined to
treat his island.   Taxes were increased, the army
was reorganized, and preparations were set on foot
for the conquest of Sicily.   To gain popularity with
the Neapolitans they abrogated some of the more
obnoxious decrees of Murat's predecessor, and they
further employed all their arts to blacken his memory,
so that they would by contrast appear the better
rulers.

But Napoleon nipped this scheme in the bud at

CAROLINE MURAT
(*née* BONAPARTE)

once. Every day brought fresh thunders from Paris.
The Emperor sent furious orders forbidding certain
measures, enjoining others, until it became very
evident that he was determined to rule Naples himself, although he was content to allow Murat to bear
the title and honours of King. Poor Murat could
do nothing right. Any well-advised action on his
part was looked upon as potential treason, while any
failure called forth tornadoes of wrath from Paris.
When, by a well-planned raid, he captured Capri
from Sir Hudson Lowe, he was actually censured
for informing the Emperor through the Ministry of
Foreign Affairs instead of through the Ministry for
War! Murat and Caroline chafed against their
bonds, but while the Empire stood firm they were
powerless.

Meanwhile, Pauline and Elise, although not as
successful as Caroline, had nevertheless attained to
some measure of sovereignty. Elise contrived for
the greater part of the time to have her dullard
husband sent away on various duties, while she herself flirted gaily with every man she could. As a
matter of fact, her flirting was never so serious as was
her sisters'; she had another outlet for her ingenuity
in that she was passionately devoted to the stage and
to all connected with it. She visited the theatre as
often as she could; she read plays in hundreds, and
she indulged in amateur theatricals whenever possible.
When Italy was being parcelled out into fiefs by
Napoleon, she prevailed on her brother to allot to
her the principality of Piombino in full sovereignty,
and later she contrived to have Lucca added to her
little state. Here she settled down for a time, with
all the paraphernalia of sovereignty, equerries,
chamberlains, ladies-in-waiting, and especially a
Court troupe of actors. Baciocchi, her husband, had
indeed been given the title of Prince of Piombino,
but Elise alone had been given the principality.

Baciocchi was merely his wife's subject, and Elise
made the most of it.   He could never worry her
again, for Elise allotted him apartments far distant
from her own, and never saw him without a third
person being present.   Scandal said that other men
were allowed greater privileges, but there is nothing
very definite from which one may draw reliable
conclusions.

Soon Elise received further promotion. Napoleon
cast a covetous eye upon the kingdom of Etruria
which had set up in 1802, and by treaty with Spain
he arranged to give the widowed Queen of Etruria
(a Spanish princess) a new kingdom of Northern
Lusitania in exchange.   That this new kingdom was
to be carved out of Portugal troubled him not at all;
he even promised to make Godoy (First Minister of
Spain) Prince of the Algarve, another Portuguese
district.   He had very little intention of fulfilling
either promise, but they enabled him to send Junot
marching hotfoot on Lisbon, and to annex Tuscany
to the Empire.   Elise seized her opportunity.   By
cajolery and blandishment she persuaded Napoleon
to erect Tuscany into a government-general, and to
confer upon her the ruling power with the title of
Grand Duchess of Tuscany.   Poor Baciocchi was
appointed general of division in command of the
French garrison.   Elise settled down in the Pitti
palace at Florence, and proceeded to rule the cradle
of the Renaissance, the erstwhile domain of the
Medicis, as thoroughly as her brother would allow
her.

Pauline's widowhood ended in a much more
splendid match than was made by any of the other
Bonapartes.   She took as her second husband Prince
Camillo Borghese, the head of one of the most
renowned houses of Italy.   The marriage was not
a success (no Bonaparte marriage was, at that time),
but Borghese's wealth and the presents Napoleon

heaped upon her enabled Pauline to indulge every whim of which she was capable. Proud of her reputation as the most beautiful woman of the time, she did all she could to enhance and set off her beauty. Like Poppæa, she bathed every day in milk—a hot milk bath followed by a cold milk shower. She surrounded herself with negro servants and dwarfs, by way of contrast, and her extravagances and wanton waste of money were the talk of the whole Empire. Canova carved her statue, and despite his cold classicism we can still perceive in that recumbent, self-satisfied figure the fiery, tempestuous woman who was once Pauline. Her posing semi-nude, even to such a sculptor as Canova, called forth a storm of comment from a gossip-loving Empire. The tale was told that when Pauline was asked if she did not feel uncomfortable, posing half-dressed, she replied, " Oh no, there was a fire in the room."

When Elise received Piombino, Pauline begged Guastalla from Napoleon, and as Duchess she, too, held sovereignty. Borghese was made Governor-General of the Piedmontese departments, and was sent to Turin with an enormous Civil List to play the part of a semi-royalty, and to reconcile the Piedmontese to the loss of their Sardinian king. Such a task was naturally agreeable to Pauline, and in Turin she and Borghese did their best to astonish the provincials with a series of fêtes of unheard-of opulence. Pauline was the most talked about of all Bonaparte's sisters ; the voice of adulation praised her beauty ; the voice of vituperation hinted frightful things about her morals. She was accused of hideous vices, of too great an affection for her brothers, of a lunatic passion for various men. Pauline apparently did not mind. She went gaily on through life, quarrelling with Borghese, spending money like water, indulging in hectic episodes with artists and soldiers, and

generally recalling to mind the old days of the
Borgias and the Viscontis.

With the publication of the fate of Napoleon's
Russian expedition a shudder ran through the
Empire.   Murat, whom Napoleon had left in command of the wreck of the Grand Army, deserted his
charge and rushed home so as to be at hand to
preserve his own kingdom should the Empire fall.
Prussia became Russia's ally.   Sweden, under Bernadotte, had already done the same.   Napoleon made
a gigantic effort; in three months he raised and
equipped an army of three hundred thousand men;
he beat back the Allies, winning victories at Lützen
and Bautzen; for a space it seemed as if he would
regain his old European domination.   Consequently
the pendulum of his allies' attitude swung back once
more towards faithfulness, and Murat left Naples
once more to command the cavalry of the Grand
Army.   But already Caroline and he had negotiated
a secret convention with Austria by which he would
declare war on France if called upon to do so.   Elise
in Tuscany had decided to join him, although,
unfortunately for her, she extracted no definite
promise from Austria that she would retain her
throne.

Thus, while Murat was fighting for the Grand
Army, leading charges made by fifty and seventy
squadrons at a time, and capturing twelve thousand
Austrian prisoners in a single battle, his wife in
Naples was assuring Austria of his devotion to
Austria; she was recruiting the Neapolitan army to
the utmost, and, while not actually moving against
France, she was refusing to allow a single Neapolitan
battalion to go to Napoleon's help.   Then came the
French defeats of 1813, culminating in the disaster
of Leipzig.   It was obvious that the Empire could
not endure much longer.   Bavaria, Baden, Würtemberg, all turned against Napoleon, and Murat realized

that if he delayed further the Allies would not have
so pressing a need for his aid, and he would be
unable to secure his throne by his treachery. Without further hesitation he left the beaten Emperor,
hurried across Europe through the first snows of
autumn, and reached Naples early in November.
The Neapolitan army was at last going to advance.

The advance was a very slow and cautious one.
Eugène de Beauharnais, Viceroy of Italy, was
fighting fiercely in Venetia against the Austrians.
Tempting offers were made to him by the Allies,
but he refused them; his dignified replies are
worthy of Bayard or Francis I. But Murat and
his Neapolitans were moving steadily northward;
even now he had made no public declaration as to
which side he was on, and in private he and Caroline
were assuring Eugène, Napoleon and the Austrians
at one and the same time of their unfailing support.
Nor was this all. They were further intriguing
with the infant United Italy party in an endeavour
to increase their dominion in that way; while in
addition they had made some sort of agreement with
Elise Bonaparte in Tuscany. It would be hard to
discover anywhere in history an equally loathsome
example of double-dealing.

Murat occupied the Papal States, Tuscany, and
portions of the Kingdom of Italy, but he still
refrained from making any open attack on either
French or Austrians. Not until March 6th, 1814,
when he received from Caroline definite news of the
certainty of the fall of the Empire, did he attack
Eugène's forces. He achieved little, and after two
fierce little skirmishes he subsided once more into
inaction. At last official intimation of Napoleon's
fall came to hand, and, abandoning Elise to her fate,
Murat returned to Naples. Further diplomacy confirmed him in his possession of Naples; the only
person concerned who kept to his pledged word in

all the intricacies of the negotiations was Francis of
Austria.

Thus 1815 found Napoleon's three sisters in very
different situations. Caroline was still a Queen;
Elise, turned out of Tuscany by the Austrians, was
a pensioner on her bounty; while Pauline, who alone
had remained faithful to her brother, was living with
Napoleon at Elba. Suddenly there came another
dramatic change, for Napoleon escaped from Elba,
and within a few days was once more Emperor of
the French. Italy was again plunged into a ferment.
Murat and Caroline were naturally anxious, for they
could not expect that Napoleon would forgive their
black treachery of the year before, while it was only
too obvious that not a single country in Europe
retained any interest in their possession of the
throne of Naples. In these circumstances Murat
took the first heroic decision of his life, and decided
to cut the Gordian knot by force of arms. He
declared war against Austria, proclaimed a United
Italy, and with fifty thousand men he marched
northward to establish himself as King of Italy. It
was a vain effort. The Neapolitan army was a
wretched force, and Murat himself was worse than
useless in independent command. The Austrian
army hurriedly concentrated, defeated Murat in
one or two minor actions, and finally utterly routed
him at Tolentino. The Neapolitans deserted in
thousands, and Murat re-entered his dominions with
only five thousand men left. The Austrians followed
him up remorselessly; the Sicilians were preparing
an expedition against him; and all that was left for
Murat to do was to abdicate and fly for his life.

Caroline was successful in obtaining the protection of Francis of Austria, and she soon went
off to settle down in Austria with a pension and
a residence. Murat had reached France, and for
some weeks he was in hiding in Marseilles. After

Waterloo he left by sea to join his wife, but on his way he changed his mind and took his second heroic decision. Napoleon had regained France simply by appearing in person before his army; why should not Murat regain Naples in the same way? Murat landed with a score of companions at Pizzo in Calabria, and marched into the market place with his escort shouting "Long live King Joachim!" For a moment there was an astonished silence, and then the townspeople fell on the little party. Not for nothing had Murat decorated every mile of every road in Calabria with a gallows from which hung captured bandits; every soul in Pizzo must have had a blood feud with their late King. Battered with sticks and stones, Murat was seized and flung into prison, and five days later he was tried and shot.

Murat's attempt was the last spurt of the Napoleonic feeling for a long period. Not until, with the passage of years, the Legend had been built up, do we hear of any surprising action or heroic deed. Europe sank into a slough of inaction, crushed down by the weight of the Holy Alliance and the burden of accumulated debts. The most typical action of a dull generation was the establishment on the throne of France of fat, pathetic, bourgeois Louis Philippe as King of the French. It was a safe thing to do, and Louis Philippe and his Amelia did their best to make it remain safe. No risks were taken until the movement of 1848. Happiness has no history, and there is precious little history about the period 1815-48. Had the Holy Alliance had its way, there would be even less. Somehow one cannot help feeling that the dullness of the period is the dullness of unhappiness. It was the time when "order reigned in Warsaw," when little children died in droves in English factories, when in Naples the negation of God was erected into a system of government. Historians may sneer

at the ineffectiveness of the Napoléonides; they
may point to a pillaged, blood-drenched Europe
writhing under the heel of a Corsican Emperor;
they can draw horrible pictures of the sacks of
Lübeck or Badajoz, but they are unconvincing
when they attempt to prove that there was more
unhappiness under the Empire than under the Holy
Alliance. Peace has its defeats as well as war.

This digression may be unpardonable, but it was
nevertheless inevitable. Let us minimize our error,
even if we cannot repair it, by turning back to the
consideration of three fair and frail women whom we
left thrust back unwillingly into a private station of
life. One of them did not long survive the calamities of 1814. This was Elise. The Allies refused
her request to join Napoleon at St. Helena, and she
lived quietly in Italy until her death in 1820. She
was only forty-two when she died. Pauline had the
advantage over her sisters of having a husband whose
position was independent of the Empire. Prince
Borghese was a very considerable person in Rome,
and Pauline for some time was a leading figure in
Italian society. It did not last long, however. She
quarrelled with her husband; her beauty left her;
Austrian, French and Papal surveillance worried
her, and she died in 1825.

Caroline, the most capable and cold-hearted of
all the Bonapartes, after Napoleon, bore her troubles
with more dignity and for a much longer time. As
the Countess of Lipona (an anagram of Napoli) she
lived for some time in Austria; she travelled rest-
lessly about; she seemed in fact to have completely
recovered from the shock of the loss of her husband
and her throne, when at last a whole series of deaths
broke down her reserve and shortened her life.
Pauline and Elise, as has been said, were already
dead; in 1832 the Prince Imperial (Napoleon II.)
died at Vienna; Prince Borghese died in the same

year. Another brother-in-law, Baciocchi, died in 1834; Catherine of Westphalia, her best beloved sister-in-law, died in 1835, and then in 1836 Madame Mère, her stern but adored mother, also died. Caroline endured her loneliness for a little while longer, but she died in 1839. Even she, almost the last of her generation, was only fifty-six at her death.

None of the Bonaparte family was as long-lived as Napoleon's mother. Maria Letizia Ramolino was certainly one of the greatest women of the period. Elise Bonaparte might be called the Semiramis of Italy; Caroline might intrigue for Empires; Pauline might be the most beautiful woman of France; but their mother combined all their good qualities with very few of their bad ones. To bring up a family of eight children thoroughly well on an income of less than one hundred pounds a year in a revolution-torn country like Corsica is in itself a remarkable feat, though hardly likely in unfavourable circumstances to gain mention in history, but to do it when handicapped by a husband like Carlo Bonaparte is more remarkable still. The strain of those dreadful years in Ajaccio would have broken down anyone of stuff less stern than Maria Letizia's; pitched battles were fought in the streets outside the Bonapartes' house; three-quarters of Corsica were at feud with the Bonapartes and the party they represented; death threatened them all at different times, while all the time a most bitter, grinding poverty harried them unmercifully.

Maria Letizia came through the ordeal unbroken in body or spirit. Even Napoleon's fierce pride humbled itself before her, and her other children were her slaves. But she had a woman's weaknesses as well as a man's strength. She was bitterly jealous of her daughter-in-law Josephine; she was bigoted in church matters; and she fought like a tigress in

I

the cause of whichever of her children was experiencing misfortune.   When Lucien left France in disgrace in consequence of his marriage to Madame Jouberthon, his mother strove desperately hard to re-establish him.   She went to Italy to be near him, and endeavoured, by absenting herself at the time of the coronation, to force Napoleon to recall Lucien and herself together.   However, her great son outwitted her on this occasion, for he dispensed with her presence, and yet arranged with David the artist for her portrait to appear along with the other French dignitaries in the celebrated picture of the coronation.

Letizia had a very good opinion of her own position.   When Napoleon became Emperor, and made his brothers and sisters Imperial Highnesses, she demanded some greater title for herself. Napoleon was in a quandary, for on consulting precedents he found that no French king's mother had ever been given any such honour if she had never been queen. Letizia insisted, and, almost at his wits' end, Napoleon at last gave her a singular dignity.   He awarded her the same position and precedence as used to be given under the Bourbons to the wife of the king's second son.   The king's second son was Monsieur, and his wife was Madame. Letizia was named Madame, and as a subsidiary title she was called Mère de S.M. l'Empéreur et Roi. Almost at once the titles were merged together in common speech, and Letizia was called Madame Mère everywhere except at strict official gatherings.

By the time that the Empire was firmly founded, and all her children except Lucien were seated on thrones, Letizia was able to give free rein to the passion which came only second with her to her love for her children.   It is said that shipwrecked sailors who have been starved for a long time cannot help, after being rescued, hoarding fragments of food for

fear of another period of famine. With Madame
Mère a similar state of affairs prevailed. She had
felt the pinch of poverty for fifty years, and in no
circumstances could she endure it again. She still
lived as cheaply as she could, and she saved her
money like a miser. She coaxed Napoleon into
giving her an annual income of a million francs, and
she did not spend a quarter of it. She did her best
to obtain a sovereignty for herself, not that she
wanted to rule, but because she could sell the fief
back to the French and invest the proceeds. She
made money by acute speculation. She clung like
grim death to every sou which came within her reach.

Yet avarice pure and simple was not the sole
motive of her actions. Just as a prophet has no
honour in his own country, so the Emperor and the
Kings and Princesses who were her children still
seemed to be children to her, and all their talk of
sovereignty was little better than childish prattling.
She did not believe for one moment that the Empire
could long endure, and in this her judgment was
more acute than that of the majority of European
statesmen. Wellington, as early as 1809, had seen
through the shams and pretences of the glittering
Empire, but few other men, not even Metternich,
agreed with him at that time. But Madame Mère
saw the end long before it came, and it was against
that time of need that she saved so avariciously.
Her judgment was proved accurate, and her savings
proved useful in 1814.

In 1802 she had befriended Lucien; in 1805,
Jerome; in 1810, Louis; now the greatest of her
sons had met with adversity, and Letizia rushed to
his assistance. She shared his exile in Elba, and
from her own purse she provided the money which
enabled him to maintain his Lilliputian court. She
was by his side during the Hundred Days, and after
he had been sent to St. Helena she returned to Italy

and resumed the headship of the family.   Her wealth as well as her marvellous personality assured her the respect of her sons and daughters.   The death of the Prince Imperial in 1832 was a terrible shock to her; she had long been looking to him to restore the fame of the exiled house, and she had arranged to leave him all her money and papers.   She did not long survive his death, but died in 1836, at the age of eighty-six.

She lies buried in Ajaccio, and the inscription over her tomb can still make the casual tourist catch his breath, and still makes the blood of Corsican youth run a little faster—

MARIA LETIZIA RAMOLINO BONAPARTE.

MATER REGUM.

CHAPTER XII

STARS OF LESSER MAGNITUDE

"BAD troops do not exist," said Napoleon on one occasion. "There are only bad officers." Napoleon did his best therefore to find good officers, and trusted that the rank and file would through them become good soldiers. And yet, was he successful either in his end or in his method? The army of 1796, which he did not train, was timid in retreat though terrible in advance. The men were fanatics, and similar strengths and weaknesses are typical of fanatics in large bodies. In 1800 Napoleon had an army which he could manœuvre in line, and which bore the dreadful strain of Marengo without breaking. Half the men in the ranks, however, were untrained boys, who, as Napoleon's despatches tell us, were ignorant a few days before the battle as to which eye they should use to aim their muskets. Marengo was largely a personal triumph for Napoleon; it was his vehement encouragement, coupled with the confident expectation of Desaix' arrival, which held the men together during that long-drawn agony.

The peace which followed Hohenlinden gave Napoleon a chance to train an army as he wished, and the Austerlitz campaign found him at the head of an army of two hundred thousand men, half of them veterans, all of them of very considerable length of service, who were to a man inspired with

133

the utmost enthusiasm for him and for the Empire. Yet at Austerlitz the line was abandoned almost entirely in favour of the column; the columns showed evident signs of disintegration even when victorious. It was already a little obvious that the Imperial armies were only adapted to a furious offensive effort, and that failure of this effort meant unlimited catastrophe.   At Jena the Prussians were too heavily outnumbered to offer any serious resistance, but at Eylau the French army was only saved from destruction after the failure of their first offensive by the fact that Napoleon held ready at hand eighteen thousand cavalry, and by the constitutional sluggishness of the Russian army.

Friedland offered the last example of a really heroic defensive by an Imperial force, but the soul of that defensive was Lannes.   Few other men could have held a French army corps together against superior forces as did Lannes on that fateful anniversary of Marengo.   After Friedland we find the French army growing progressively poorer and more unreliable.   We read of panics at Wagram, of the introduction of regimental artillery to give the infantry confidence, of shameless skulking on the field of battle and of heavy desertion while on the march.   Discipline was fading at the same time as devotion to the Emperor was losing some of its force.   In the Russian campaign of 1812 the Grand Army had barely crossed the frontier before it began to go to pieces.   Napoleon could not trust his men to manœuvre at Borodino, and in consequence he had to rely on frontal attacks made against elaborate fieldworks defended by the most stubborn of all Continental infantry.   At the crisis of the battle he refused to fling the Imperial Guard into the struggle; some thought it was because he was too far from his base to risk his best reserve; some

LETIZIA BONAPARTE
(MADAME MÈRE)

suspected Bessières of having implored him not to waste his best troops; but perhaps the reason was a more logical one. Had the Guard been sent forward and been beaten back, the whole army would have fallen back routed; at Waterloo Napoleon took the risk and lost; at Borodino he refused to take it and was satisfied with an indecisive gain.

The Grand Army perished in Russia, but in three months Napoleon raised, trained and equipped three hundred thousand more men and was for a time once more successful. Curiously enough, this raw infantry of 1813 was to all intents and purposes of greater military value than the two or three year trained infantry of 1812. The army of 1812 possessed the little knowledge proverbially dangerous, and would not willingly expose itself to sacrifice, but the novices of 1813 knew nothing of war, and suffered losses and privations which would have roused veterans to mutiny. At Lutzen Ney's corps of half-grown boys endured for hours the attack of the whole Allied force, and fought like demons in the shelter of the villages of Gorschen and Kaya. At Bautzen the French attacked with a dash and fury reminiscent of Elchingen or Saalfeld. Before Dresden they accomplished a march which easily bears comparison with anything achieved in 1796. But the decline of their fame had already begun. At the Katzbach, at Gross Beeren, at Dennewitz, the conscripts fled in panic. They had discovered by this time that a battle generally implies the sacrifice of one portion of the army while the rest gains the victory, and they were one and all determined not to be the sacrifice. At Leipzig what was left of the army of 1813 lost the greater part of its numbers—a new lesson to the effect that it is easier to surrender than to fight had been learned. Napoleon's last victorious phase, in the campaign of France in 1814, coincides with his use of a fresh army of raw conscripts, and his surrender took place when the men of the ranks had once more learnt the lessons of their predecessors.

Waterloo, the last battle of the Empire, epitomizes all these observations. The French attacked with dash, but a single reverse was sufficient to weaken the infantry so much that no support was forthcoming for the later cavalry attacks. A powerful counter-attack by the enemy brought about, not merely retreat, but unspeakable panic. Practically every battalion which had been in action broke and fled. The Guard, which had moved forward so majestically, dispersed like the merest conscripts. The only troops which held together were the reserve battalions of the Old Guard, which had not yet been engaged, and for a time Lobau's corps at Planchenoit. The Prussians after Jena were not so hopelessly disorganized as were the French after Waterloo.

Napoleon undoubtedly appreciated this weakness of his army, and this explains the reckless manner in which he sought battle at all costs, and the risks he cheerfully ran in his endeavour to get to grips with his enemy. His headlong, energetic strategy gave him the initiative, and this initiative he retained on the field of battle. Jena, Eylau, Eckmühl, Aspern, Wagram, Borodino, were all examples of a fierce tactical offensive. On the two principal occasions, at Austerlitz and Friedland, when he confined some part of his force to a dogged defensive, he saw that the generals in command were men of wide personal influence, and that the troops they led were the best available. Davout and Lannes were certainly successful. At Lützen Ney's necessarily defensive rôle was not fully fore-seen, but he was able to hold on, partly through the enthusiasm of his young men, partly through the advantage they possessed in holding the villages, and partly through Wittgenstein's bungling of the attack.

At no period in its development will Napoleon's army bear comparison with, say, the army of Cromwell, or the original force of Gustavus Adolphus, or with the army of the Third Republic. It incidentally follows that Napoleon's military achievements should be rated even higher than they usually are, seeing that the immense successes he gained were gained with inferior troops.

But if the rank and file were of this doubtful quality, it was far otherwise with the officers, and the statement of Napoleon's with which this chapter opens is therefore subject to doubt. Napoleon's method of making war support war exposed his armies, as he candidly admitted, to a loss of one half of their numbers every year, and since this loss fell far more heavily on the privates than on the officers, it followed that a very widely experienced corps of officers was built up. It was quite usual for men of good birth to serve a few months in the ranks before taking commissions; Marbot and Bugeaud are good examples of this among the younger men. Once they had gained their lieutenancy anything might happen. They might in ten years be dukes and generals, or they might still be lieutenants. The open system of promotion was stimulating, certainly, but it was undoubtedly unfair at times. Curély, who served from 1800 to 1814, and was subsequently admitted to be the best light cavalry officer in the French service, only attained his colonelcy in his last campaign. The men who received the most rapid promotion were those who had attracted Napoleon's notice in 1796 or in the Egyptian campaign. Some of these choices were highly successful, as witness the career of Davout, but others were positively harmful. Marmont was a failure, Junot was a failure,

Murat was a failure, while men of undoubted talent served in twenty campaigns without receiving promotion. Kellermann the younger fought at Waterloo with the same military rank as he had held at Marengo.   Suchet, who was one of the most successful generals of division in 1799, remained a general of division until 1811. If this was the case with the higher ranks, it must have been nearly as bad with the lower ranks.   When the rush of promotion of the Revolutionary era ended, advancement became very slow indeed. A man who was a captain at the battle of the Pyramids might well consider himself fortunate if he commanded a battalion at Ligny. Occasionally, however, the divisional generals were given their chance.   The vast expansion of the Imperial Army for the Russian campaign increased the commands of some of the Marshals to eighty or a hundred thousand men, and generals of division similarly found themselves at the head of twenty or thirty thousand. Many of them displayed talents of a very high order. St. Cyr won the battle of Polotsk, for which he received his bâton. The most remarkable example occurred at Salamanca. Here Wellington had flung himself suddenly on the over-extended Army of Portugal, had shattered one wing, and had beaten back the remainder in dire confusion; Marmont, the commander-in-chief, was badly wounded. Bonnet had hardly succeeded to the command when he was killed. Several other generals of division were struck down. The man who took over command of the fleeing mob was already wounded. He was practically unknown; he was leading a beaten army in wild retreat from the finest troops in the world. And yet he rallied that beaten army; in the course of a few hours he had them once more in hand. He faced about time and again as he toiled across the wasted Castilian plains; in a dozen fierce rearguard actions he taught the exultant English that some Frenchmen, as well as being more than men in victory, were not less than women in defeat, and he showed Wellington that every French general was not a Marmont. Every morning found his army posted in some strong position; all day long the English marched by wretched roads and over thirsty plains to turn the flanks; every evening as the movement was nearing completion the French fell back to some new position where the English had to resume the whole weary business next day.   The French survived the severest defeat they had yet received in the Peninsula at English hands with astonishingly little loss; a few weeks later they had so far recovered as to thrust fiercely forward once more, and aid in driving Wellington from Madrid. The man who was responsible for this wonderful achievement deserved reward.   Bessières and Marmont had been given bâtons for much less.   A title, a marshalate, a dotation of a million francs would not have seemed too much for saving for France a kingdom, an army of forty thousand men, and dependent forces numbering a quarter of a million.   But Clausel was not made Marshal, nor Duke of Burgos. Instead he was recalled, and an inferior general, Souham, sent in his place.   Napoleon had a prejudice against " retreating generals " dating from the days of Moreau. Clausel took the affront philosophically, and fought on for his Emperor. When it was too late, his worth was recognized, and during the Hundred Days he was given the independent command of the Pyrenees. After Waterloo he fled from France with a price on his head.   Clausel went unrewarded; Murat was over-rewarded.   Their lines of conduct differed greatly.

The men who were never granted the coveted

rank of Marshal, but who did each as much for
France as any one of half the Marshals, are in
number legion. Their very names would fill a page.
Kellermann the younger has already been mentioned.
At Marengo his desperate charge at the head of the
heavy cavalry saved the day, and "set the crown of
France on Napoleon's head." But Napoleon found
it far safer and far cheaper to praise a dead man, and
he awarded the chief credit to the slain Desaix.
D'Hautpoult died at the head of his Cuirassiers at
Eylau, charging one army to save another. St.
Hilaire, the finest of them all, died miserably at
Essling, with the Empire reeling round him.
Lasalle, the pride of the light cavalry, the man who
captured Stettin with a few score Hussars, fell at
the head of his men in the pursuit after Wagram.
Montbrun, another Cuirassier, was killed in the
great redoubt at Borodino.

Their names are carved upon the Arc de
Triomphe, and the bourgeois peer at them with
self-satisfaction. They fell in a far less worthy
cause than did the myriad Frenchmen who died by
poison gas and shrapnel in the trenches a few years
ago. To us now it seems to be nearly blasphemy
to think in the same moment of the Moskowa and
the Marne, or to speak in the same breath of the
sieges of Verdun and of Hamburg. The Englishman turns lightly from the great names on the Arc
de Triomphe, and thinks with proud regret of the
simple inscription on an empty tomb in Whitehall.
And yet these men were the wonders of their time.
They did their duty; more cannot be said of any
man, and much less of most. They gave their
lives with a smile for a country which they adored.
Danger was as usual to them as was the air they
breathed. They gave their blood in streams; they
marched with their men into every Continental
capital. Their cowed enemies regarded them

timidly, as though they were beings from another world.   Their continued success and their overwhelming victories might well have led them to believe themselves superhuman.   And when Waterloo was fought and lost they went back to their beloved France—such of them as survived—and nursed their wounds on pensions of thirty pounds a year.

There was one general of division who attained as near as might be to a marshalate without quite achieving this last step.   He was made a duke and he gained a vast fortune.   This man was Junot.   Junot, indeed, is often stated to have received his bâton, but he never did, although he was as much a favourite of Napoleon's at one time as was Marmont.   It was Junot who at Toulon was writing a letter at Bonaparte's dictation, when a cannon-shot plunged near by and scattered earth over them.   "We need no sand to dry the ink now," laughed Junot, and from that day his future was made.   He married Mademoiselle Laurette Permon, whom Napoleon had once courted, and whose memoirs are one of the most interesting books of the period.   Junot himself served as Bonaparte's aide-de-camp all over Europe and in Egypt as well.   He received promotion steadily, and was a general of division in a very brief while.   With that rank, however, he was forced to be content, for Napoleon realized his shortcomings, while a wound in the head which he early received unbalanced him a little mentally.   The one outstanding feature of his character was his passionate devotion to Napoleon.   Napoleon was his God, and Junot served him with a faithfulness almost unexampled.   Adventures came his way with a frequency characteristic of the period.   He fell into English hands and was exchanged; he went as ambassador to Portugal and made a large fortune; he was appointed Governor of Paris, and withstood

Caroline Bonaparte's blandishments when she tried to induce him to subvert the Government. Half dead with wounds, he travelled across Europe in November, 1805, and arrived at Austerlitz on the very morning of the battle. He was again wounded heading a charge that day. In 1807 Napoleon gave him a command which he hoped would bring him fame, and a marshalate was promised in the event of success. Junot was to lead the army of Portugal from France to Lisbon; he was to capture the Portuguese royal family and the English shipping in the harbour; he was to tear down the Portuguese Government and to rule the country himself in the name of the Emperor. Junot set out with a mixed French and Spanish force numbering nearly forty thousand men. At every stage he received frantic orders from Paris demanding greater speed from him and his men. Junot did what he could. The whole valley of the Tagus was littered with the guns, dead horses and exhausted men whom he had left behind. His army was dispersed into fragments, and it was only with four hundred men at his back that Junot burst into Lisbon. The English shipping and the Portuguese royal family had fled the day before.

Junot was in a serious position. With four hundred men he had to rule a large town simmering with rebellion, but he succeeded, and held the country down while the rest of his army trailed disconsolately into Lisbon. His astonishing march had not achieved its object, and the marshal's bâton was therefore withheld. Napoleon offered some sort of consolation by creating Junot Duke of Abrantès, but there is no doubt that the disappointment weighed heavily upon him. Napoleon had meditated making Junot Duke of Nazareth, in memory of his victory during the Syrian campaign, but he had decided that it would be inadvisable, as the soldiers would call him " Junot of Nazareth."

Napoleon was not quite so far-sighted when at the same time he made Victor, at the suggestion of one of the wits of his court, Duke of Belluno. Victor was commonly called the Beau Soleil of the French Army. Napoleon's investiture made him Duke of Belle Lune.

Immediately afterwards the Spanish war broke out, and Junot found himself isolated at Lisbon. He gathered his forces together, and without any help whatever from France he maintained them and re-equipped them at the cost of unfortunate Portugal. But it was not to last long, for Wellington landed in Mondego bay, and Junot, furiously attacking him, was badly beaten at Vimiero. There followed the Convention of Cintra. By it Junot and his men were transported back to France with their arms, baggage and plunder; all that the English gained was a bloodless occupation of Portugal. It is difficult now to decide who had the best of this agreement. Certainly Napoleon thought that Junot had made a good bargain, and equally certainly the English public thought that Wellington had blundered badly.

If the Convention had not been concluded, the English would have cut Junot off from France (two hundred thousand Spanish insurgents had done that already) and would have shut him up in Lisbon. Without a doubt, Junot would have made a desperate resistance there. Masséna's holding of Genoa in 1800 might have been re-enacted, and the wretched Portuguese might have starved while Junot held out. In this event the hands of the English would have been so full that no help could have been offered to the Spanish armies; Moore's skilful thrust at Sahagun could never have been made, and the Spaniards might have met with utter annihilation. By the Convention of Cintra, France gained an immediate benefit, but England eventually gained even more.

After Vimiero, Junot's military career is one of

continued failure—failure under Masséna in the
Busaco campaign, failure under Napoleon in the
Russian campaign, until at last the Duke of Abrantès
was sent into comparative exile as Governor of
Illyria.   Here his troubles, his wounds and his dis-
appointments bore too heavily upon him.   He went
raving mad, and performed all sorts of lunatic actions
in his Illyrian province until he was removed to
France.   At Dijon he flung himself from a window
and killed himself.   Junot is one more example of
those whom Napoleon favoured, who met with
horrible ends.

But Marshals and Generals alike, Napoleon's
superior officers were nearly all distinguished by one
common failing—a dread of responsibility and a
hopeless irresolution when compelled to act on their
own initiative.   The examples of this are almost too
numerous to mention; the most striking perhaps is
Berthier's failure during the early period of the
campaign of 1809.   There are many others which had
much more important results, although at first they
seem trivial in comparison.   Thus, Dupont's surrender at Baylen, although it only involved twenty
thousand men, was one of the principal causes of the
prolongation of the Peninsular War.   Dupont
surrendered with twenty thousand men; his action
necessitated the employment in the Peninsula of
three hundred thousand men for six years afterwards.

Another incident of the same type was Vandamme's disaster at Kulm.   Vandamme was a burly,
heavy-jawed soldier of the furious and thoughtless
kind, who had learnt his trade thoroughly well by
rule of thumb, and who had made his name a byword
throughout Germany on account of his dreadful
depredations.   His boast was that he feared neither
God nor devil, and Napoleon referred to this once
when he said that Vandamme was the most valuable
of all his soldiers because he was the only one he

could employ in a war against the Infernal regions, should such a contingency arise.

In July, 1813, the Armistice of Pleisswitz had come to an end, and Austria had joined the ranks of Napoleon's enemies. The Grand Army was in Silesia when the news arrived that the Austrians were marching on Dresden. Napoleon turned back without hesitation, marched a hundred and twenty miles in four days, and by what was almost his last victory he saved the town. At the commencement of his march he had detached Vandamme with twenty thousand men to hold the passes of the Erz Gebirge against the retreating forces. The beaten Austrian army came reeling back towards them. The Emperor of Austria and the Czar of Russia were present in its ranks, and it seemed as if nothing could save them from surrender. Fortunately, perhaps, for Europe, Napoleon was unwell and did not press the pursuit as closely as he might have done, and Vandamme, who rushed into peril like a bull into the ring, without outposts, without flank guards, without any reasonable protection, was overwhelmed by forces outnumbering his by four to one, and was forced to surrender. Vandamme may have feared neither God nor devil, but he had not the brains for a command in chief, even against men.

His own honour he redeemed from all possible accusations of cowardice, when, a prisoner in Austrian hands, with all the possibilities before him of condemnation to slow death in a salt-mine or speedy death on the spot, he was led before the Czar, and he did not quail. Alexander rated him for his excesses in Prussia, and Vandamme hit back at Alexander's tender spot—his conscience. " At least I did not kill my own father," said Vandamme.

Indecision characterizes the actions of many French generals during the Empire. The most discussed case perhaps was Grouchy's hesitation at

K

Wavre during the Waterloo campaign, and this,
curiously enough, was not really hesitation. The
sole military crime of which Grouchy was guilty was
a too pedantic obedience to orders. Grouchy has
been blamed for misreading the situation and for not
marching from Wavre on Waterloo, but Napoleon
misread the situation just as badly, as his orders to
Grouchy clearly prove. Moreover, once Grouchy's
hands had been freed by the destruction of the main
French army, his actions were exceedingly bold and
competent. His retreat across the Allies' rear and
his capture of Namur were manœuvres of sound
military skill.

Grouchy's military career had been in every way
honourable throughout his life. He had ridden
bravely to destruction at the head of his dragoons
during Murat's charge at Eylau. He had fought
magnificently at Friedland and elsewhere. The
only other time when he had been in independent
command, and when he did display genuine dilatori-
ness was many years before when he had found
himself in command owing to the loss of Hoche on
the French expedition to Bantry Bay in 1796.
Grouchy's courage failed him then, and he withdrew
at the very time when his landing would have set
Ireland in an inextinguishable blaze. For a series
of quite strictly correct actions at Waterloo Grouchy
has gone down to history as a fool and a humbug,
but he was neither—to any great extent.

During the Waterloo campaign there was
certainly one example of a general being overwhelmed
by his sense of responsibility. Up to the moment
of execution not one of Napoleon's plans of attack
had been more brilliantly conceived or better
arranged. A hundred and twenty thousand men
were assembled at the crossings of the Sambre by
Charleroi without the enemy gathering more than a
hint as to what was in the air; in fact the Allies'

Intelligence completely lost sight of Gérard's corps of sixteen thousand men.   From this point, however, the arrangements rapidly grew worse and worse. Bad staff work caused delays at the crossing of the Sambre; Ney's unexpected appointment to the command of the left wing was disturbing, in that he was without a staff and his sudden elevation annoyed d'Erlon and Reille, his subordinate corps commanders.   Zieten's stubborn rearguard actions held up the French columns for a considerable time; and finally a sort of universal misunderstanding led to everyone being more or less in the dark as to the need for a determined and immediate attack.   Ney, goaded by repeated orders, at last attacked at Quatre Bras quite six hours later than he should have done, and even then he had only half his force in hand. The other half, under d'Erlon, was making its way towards him, when it was caught up by an aide-de-camp of Napoleon's, who was bearing a message to Ney requesting him to send help to the Emperor at Ligny.   The aide-de-camp, on his own responsibility, sent d'Erlon marching over towards Ligny instead of to Quatre Bras, and went on to inform Ney of his action.   Ney was furious.   Every moment the British army in front of him was being reinforced, and he was now being steadily pushed back.   He saw defeat close upon him, and he sent off a frantic order to d'Erlon to retrace his steps and march on Quatre Bras.   The order reached d'Erlon at the crisis of the battle of Ligny.   For hours a fierce and sanguinary battle had raged there, and at the crucial moment d'Erlon had appeared, like a god from a machine, with twenty thousand men on the Prussian flank.   Napoleon sent him urgent orders to attack, but the officier d'ordonnance returned disconsolate. D'Erlon had just received Ney's order and had marched back towards Quatre Bras, where he arrived just as darkness fell, two hours too late.   His sense

of responsibility did not permit him to disregard the
orders of his immediate superior, although it had lain
in his power, by disregarding them, to have dealt the
Prussian army a blow from which it could hardly
have recovered.   The attack d'Erlon should have
made was later made by six thousand weary men who
had fought all day long, and naturally did not have
the immense success d'Erlon might have achieved.

Drouet, Comte d'Erlon, had built himself up
during twenty campaigns a reputation as a skilful
and hard-fighting officer.   He was neither a poltroon
nor congenitally weak-minded; what was the matter
with him was that he had fought twenty campaigns
under Napoleon.   The brilliance of the Emperor and
the implicit, blind obedience he demanded had
weakened d'Erlon's initiative past all reckoning.   It
is interesting to compare d'Erlon's action at Ligny
with Lannes' at Friedland, or with the daring of the
subordinate Prussian officers at Mars-la-Tour and at
Gravelotte in 1870.

And yet one cannot help but think, on reading
military history, that the Lannes and the Davouts
of this world are astonishingly few when compared
with the d'Erlons and the Duponts.   Military history
is a history of blunders, fortunate or unfortunate.
Men are found everywhere in control of the lives
and destinies of ten, twenty, a hundred thousand
men, and completely unable even to expend them in
an efficient manner.   On reading of the fumbling
campaigns of Schwartzenberg, of Carlo Alberto, of
Napoleon III., or even of wars waged more recently
still, and of which we ourselves have had experience,
one cannot help feeling overwhelming pity at the
thought of the wretched men—every one of them as
full of life as you or I—who were called upon to lay
down everything at the call of duty or patriotism—
and to lay down everything *uselessly*.   The argument
against war which appeals most to those who may

have to take part in it is not so much that it is
expensive or that it costs lives, but that it is so
blightingly inefficient. To die because one's country
is in need, that is one thing ; but to die because one's
commanding officer has bad dreams, is quite another
matter.

But the armies of Napoleon were at least free
from a horrible slur which has been cast upon other
armies. We cannot find anywhere any hint that the
officers did not do all their duty as far as they
visualized it. On going into action the men did not
shout " Les epaulettes en avant " as did the army
of the Second Empire at Solferino. No officer of
Napoleon's ever wasted his men's lives to gratify his
own pride, in the way that English marines died at
Trafalgar. It was said with pride of an officer of
Marlborough's that he always said, " Come on " not
" Go on " to his men. The same could be said of
every one of the higher officers of the army of the
First Empire. The hundreds of volumes of memoirs
written by Napoleon's men teem with examples
(grudgingly given, in some cases) of valour, but there
is hardly one case where an Imperial officer is accused
of cowardice, or even of shirking. The officers bore
exactly the same hardships as did the men, and the
friendship and trust which existed between the rank
and file and the commissioned officers of the army
of the First Empire has never been excelled in any
other army in history.

A simple calculation at any Napoleonic battle will
show that the number of generals killed is proportion-
ate to that of the privates, while of the twenty-four
Marshals of the Empire who fought after the
inauguration, three—Lannes, Bessières and Poniatowski—were killed in action, and all the others were
wounded at various times. Napoleon himself, as is
well known, was wounded during the fighting round
Ratisbon in 1809, and Duroc, his trusted Grand

Marshal of the Palace, was struck down at his side by a stray cannon shot at Bautzen in 1813, and died an hour later in horrible agony.

The facts about the Imperial army are curiously contradictory. The men were devoted to Napoleon, but their devotion did not hold them together in moments of panic. The officers were experienced in all the details of war, but for all their experience they lost touch with the Prussian army during the vital period following Ligny. Napoleon had laid down as essential various rules of strategy—but he departed from them during the autumn campaign of 1813. Nothing seems consistent or satisfactory during the whole period.

Yet there are hundreds upon hundreds of incidents of which one cannot read without a thrill. Cambronne at Waterloo replying with a curse when called upon to surrender in the face of certain destruction; the Red Lancers of the Guard gaining the Somo Sierra in the teeth of a tempest of cannon shot; the conscripts of 1814, in sabots and blouses, facing undaunted the savage enemy cavalry at Champaubert; Ney rallying the rearguard during the retreat from Moscow; Kellermann charging an army at Quatre Bras; the engineers dying gladly to save the army at the Beresina; all these incidents are worthy to be remembered with pride, and almost blot out the memory of the hideous ferocity of these self-same men in Spain, in Germany and in Russia.

It is the fate of the Emperor and the Grand Army to be equally at the mercy of the panegyrics of the admirer and the insults of anyone who chooses to inveigh against them.

ELISE BACCIOCHI
(*née* BONAPARTE)

CHAPTER XIII

WOMEN

IT would be as easy to omit all mention of
Napoleon's mistresses in a serious history as it
would be difficult to omit the king's mistresses
from a history of Louis le Grand or Louis le Bien-
Aimé. Napoleon was not the man to allow his policy
to be influenced by women. Not one of the many
with whom he came into contact could boast that
she had deflected him one hairbreadth from the path
he had mapped for himself. Not all Josephine's
tears could save the life of the young d'Enghien;
not all Walewska's pleading could re-establish the
kingdom of Poland.

" Adultery," said Napoleon, " is a sofa affair,"
and he was speaking for once in all honesty. He
was a man blessed with a vast personality, a vast
power and a vast income, and it is unusual for a man
with these three to go long a-suing. Moreover, if
the lady who attracted his attention proved recal-
citrant, Napoleon rarely pleaded; he raised his offer,
and in the event of a further refusal he turned
away without a sigh and forgot all about her. That
indicates Napoleon's attitude towards women.

There were, as a matter of fact, one or two whom
he honoured by more lover-like attentions. Josephine cost him many bitter hours of self-reproach;
Walewska he sought long and earnestly; he displayed
every sign of attachment towards Marie Louise.

151

Yet not merely these three, but every woman who granted him favours received in return immense gifts, and, if she desired it, a husband whose path to promotion was made specially easy.   The women who flit into and then out of Napoleon's life seem to be without number, but the gossip of a thousand memoirs, and the hints of a thousand letters, combined with the painstaking care of a crowd of patient inquirers, have brought them all under notice at some time or other.   And yet the most elaborate research can only prove that there was one woman who might perhaps have given much to Bonaparte before his meeting with Josephine, and that was a street-walker of the Palais Royal.   This tiny incident is hinted at in a letter written by Bonaparte at the age of eighteen.

After this, we find nothing of the same nature for another nine years.   Napoleon was too busy and too desperately poor to trouble about such things. He flirted with Laurette Permon, who later became Madame Junot, Duchesse d'Abrantès; with his sister-in-law, Désirée Clary, afterwards Madame Bernadotte, Princess of Ponte Corvo and Queen of Sweden and Norway; and with a few young women of good social position whom he met while serving as a junior officer of artillery at Valence.   That is all.   He came to Josephine heartwhole and inexperienced, and he lavished upon her during the first feverish months of his married life all the stored-up passion of a man of twenty-six.   Josephine baulked and thwarted this passion by her delay in joining him while he was conquering Italy, by her petty flirtations with Charles and others, and by the general light-mindedness of her behaviour; from that time forth Napoleon became passionless towards all women. Some he liked, and some he even admired, as far as it was in his nature to admire anyone, but for none did he ever exhibit the uncontrollable desire which

for that brief space he had felt for Josephine.
Unfaithfulness to her, which he would once have
regarded as treason, he now thought of merely as
necessary to a man of mature age.

However, throughout the years 1796 and 1797
one cannot find any proof of genuine inconstancy.
It was only in 1798, when Napoleon found himself
the unrestrained ruler of Egypt, with the whole East
apparently at his feet, that he left the narrow path of
strict physical virtue. The native ladies did not
appeal to him, and he turned with disgust from their
over opulent charms. The same cannot be said of
some of his officers, a few of whom actually married
Egyptian beauties and later brought them back to
France. Menou, who succeeded to the chief command after Napoleon's departure and Kléber's
assassination, was one of these. Others, again,
married and settled down in Egypt after the
evacuation. Their descendants were supporters of
Mehemet Ali, and even nowadays many rich
Egyptian proprietors can trace back their descent
to a Frankish ancestor who became a Mohammedan
a hundred and twenty years ago.

But although, as has been said, Napoleon found
no charms behind the yashmaks, the possibilities
were by no means exhausted, as his aides-de-camp
hastened to point out to him. A few Frenchwomen,
by donning male attire, had evaded the strict regulation that no women should accompany the Army of
the Orient. The most attractive of these was
Marguèrite Pauline, wife of a lieutenant of Chasseurs, by name Fourès. To a Commander-in-Chief
all things are possible, and young Fourès was packed
off in one of the frigates which had escaped from the
disaster of the Nile with orders to carry despatches
to the Directory. The night of his departure
Madame Fourès (la Bellîlote, as she was called, from
her maiden name of Belleisle) was entertained by

Napoleon at a gay little dinner party; the proceedings, however, were cut short by the General upsetting iced water over her dress and carrying her off under the pretext of having the damage attended to.

After this la Bellilote was established in a Cairo palace close to General Headquarters, and the little idyll seemed to be progressing famously when a most indignant intruder in the person of Lieutenant Fourès appeared on the scene. He had been captured by the English on his way to Italy, and had been returned for the express purpose of inconveniencing the Général-en-chef. The English were, however, doomed to disappointment, for Napoleon, exercising his dictatorial powers, had a divorce pronounced between Fourès and his wife, and then sent the wretched man back once more to France. From this time forth la Bellilote had an almost regal dominion in Cairo. The finest silks in the land were confiscated for her adornment, and she drove about the streets amid cries from the soldiers of " Vive la Générale " and " Vive Clioupatre! " At times she even appeared on horseback in a general's uniform and cocked hat. The whole proceeding savours of some of the doings of the early Roman Emperors. Suetonius tells us very similar stories of Nero and Caligula. Little adverse comment was caused among the French; it was a very usual thing during the Revolutionary era for officers to be accompanied by women in this fashion. Some women even served generals as aides-de-camp and orderlies, while the Army of Portugal during 1810-11 was frequently hindered because Masséna, commanding, had his *chère amie* with him.

Madame Fourès' experience of the delights of being the left-handed queen of the uncrowned king of an unacknowledged kingdom was not destined to endure long; Napoleon returned to France, and she, following him, by his orders, as soon as possible, fell into the hands of the English just as her husband had done. When at last she reached France Bonaparte refused to see her, for he was now reconciled to Josephine, besides being First Consul and having to be careful of his moral reputation. Napoleon did whatever else he could for her; he gave her large sums of money, bought her houses, and secured a new husband for her, whose agreement he ensured by means of valuable appointments under the Ministry of Foreign Affairs.

Napoleon and la Bellilote never met again; after 1815 she eloped with another man, built up a substantial fortune in the South American trade, and finally died quite in the odour of sanctity at the venerable age of ninety-one.

On Bonaparte's return to France Josephine had contrived to win him once more to her, despite the efforts of his family, and his own half-determination to end the business there and then, but matters were never the same between them. Napoleon indulged more and more frequently in petty amours with various women, and Josephine, instead of appreciating her helplessness, as is the more usual way with queens and empresses, caused frequent furious scenes by spying on his actions and upbraiding him when any rumour came to her notice. Napoleon cared no whit; he was, moreover, able, by virtue of his supreme power, frequently to ensure that Josephine knew nothing of his infidelity. In 1800 he was peculiarly successful in this way. Marengo had been fought and won, and the First Consul was enjoying, at Milan, the fruits of his dramatic success. The most eminent contralto of the time, Grassini, sang at concerts hurriedly arranged in his honour. Grassini had endeavoured to force herself on his notice three years before, without success, for Josephine held power over him then. The circumstances were different now, and Napoleon, his

Italian temperament inexpressibly charmed by her magnificent voice, honoured her by a summons to his apartments. She obeyed gladly; she came at his request to Paris; and finally Napoleon had the effrontery to command her to sing at the thanksgiving festival in the Invalides for the Marengo campaign, where he appeared accompanied by his wife and by all the notabilities of the Consulate. Later she appeared at the Théâtre de la République, and was given a large allowance, both publicly as a singer and secretly as a friend of Napoleon's. The arrangement ended abruptly, for Grassini was detected in an intrigue with an Italian musician, and left France for a Continental tour.

It was not till 1807 that she returned, and although Napoleon never renewed the old relationship, he gave her an official title, a large salary and employment under his Bureau of Music.

Grassini spent the rest of her days mainly in Paris, and she enjoyed a vast reputation all her life. Money troubles, due to her passion for gambling, and wild adventures of the heart, engaged most of her attention. It has even been said that after Waterloo she condescended to grant Wellington the same favours as Napoleon had enjoyed thirteen years before. Despite the obvious bias of many of the witnesses, the evidence to this end seems conclusive. If it really was true, then Grassini might claim a distinction as notable as Alava's, who was the only man who fought both at Trafalgar and at Waterloo.

After Grassini passed out of Napoleon's life, a long period ensued during which no woman received the Emperor's favour for any continuous length of time. At intervals various hooded figures slipped through the postern door of the Tuileries, past Roustam the Mameluke, and through a secret passage to the Imperial apartments, but the visits were irregular and were merely the results of passing

whims on the part of the Emperor. Not one of the
women concerned had need of much pressure to
become agreeable to the invitations brought them by
Duroc, the faithful Grand Marshal of the Palace.
They were actresses mainly, and since most of them
appeared at theatres managed or subsidized by the
Government, Napoleon, if not their direct employer,
had in his gift important acting parts and desirable
salaries. Many of them were already the mistresses
of dandies of the town, and some of them passed on
to act in the same capacity for various crowned heads
of Europe, while one was actually requested by a
powerful party in Russia to win Alexander the Czar
from an objectionable *chère amie* so that he might
return to the Czarina!

Napoleon did all he could to keep these liaisons
secret, but he was rarely successful. The women
boasted far and wide of their success, and it is likely
that many of those who boasted had nothing to boast
about. Some even went so far as to publish their
memoirs after the Restoration, and to make capital
of their own dishonour. Another factor which
militated against secrecy was Josephine's jealousy.
Josephine, with the spectre of divorce always before
her eyes, was in continual terror lest Napoleon should
experience a lasting attachment for one of his stray
lights o' love. Consequently she spied upon him
incessantly, battered on his locked doors, wrote
frantic appeals to her friends for help and information, and generally acted with less than her usual
dignity. Napoleon disregarded her appeals, and
stormed back at her whenever she ventured to
remonstrate. He was above all law, he declared, and
he would allow no human being to judge his actions.
Nevertheless, he took care to interfere with the most
intimate affairs of all his friends. He tried to bully
Berthier, his trusted Chief of Staff, into separating
from the lady with whom he had lived for years. At

first it seemed as if he was successful, and he consoled his friend by giving him as wife a Princess of the royal House of Bavaria. However, Berthier contrived to obtain his young bride's agreement to the presence of the other lady, and the three of them ran a perfectly happy *ménage à trois* for the rest of his life. Napoleon meddled with many other people's domestic affairs, and it is darkly hinted that Talleyrand's enmity for the Emperor began when Napoleon first disturbed the tranquillity which existed between the great diplomat and Madame Grand.

The Emperor continued serenely on his way, acting up to his dictum that women were merely incidents in a man's life. His Court was thronged with greedily ambitious women who threw themselves in his path at every opportunity. At the least hint of a preference on his part, officious courtiers hurried to assist in the negotiations in the hope either of favour or perquisites. The astonishing thing is that the list of the chosen is not many times longer. These intrigues all ran much the same course—a brief partnership, generally without a hint of affection on either side; a minor place in Court for the lady; then a marriage was arranged, an ample dowry provided by the Emperor, and the incident was closed. Not merely did people endeavour to gain their private ends in this manner, but even political parties made use of similar tools. During the Consulate the Bourbons despatched a lady to Paris for the sole purpose of ensnaring Bonaparte, and it is hinted that Metternich endeavoured to place a friend at Court in the same fashion. The great example of this political manoeuvre, however, occurs later.

But before Madame Walewska's name, even, was known to Napoleon, he formed an attachment of some slight historical importance. Eléonore Denuelle was an exceedingly beautiful girl, daughter of parents of a doubtful mode of life, who had been

educated at Madame Campan's famous school along
with Caroline Bonaparte and various other great
ladies of the Court. Her parents designed a great
marriage for her, but they met with poor success,
for a certain graceless ex-officer, by name Revel,
succeeded in making her believe that he was a
good match, and the couple were married early in
1805. Revel believed that Eléonore was an heiress;
Eléonore believed that Revel was a rich man; they
were both of them woefully disappointed, and
separated after two months of married life. Eléonore
in despair applied for help to Caroline Murat, and
received a minor post in that princess's household.
Napoleon noticed her in January, 1806, and from
that time the affair moved rapidly, for in February
Eléonore applied for a divorce from Revel (who was
now in gaol), and in December a son was born to
her whose father, almost without a doubt, was
Napoleon.

By the time of his birth, however, Napoleon had
formed a new attachment, and Eléonore was never
again admitted to his rooms. Napoleon saw that
both his son and his ex-mistress were suitably provided for; he settled a thousand pounds a year on
Eléonore and married her to a prominent politician
(a Monsieur Augier), while he invested large sums
of money in trust for her son, Léon. He further
mentioned him in his will. Eléonore's later career
was unlucky; her second husband died, a prisoner in
Russian hands, and when she married for a third
time she was blackmailed for the rest of her life by
her first husband and by her scapegrace illegitimate
son. Léon ruined all his chances of success in life
by his reckless way of living. He gambled away all
he possessed, and then lived on what small sums he
could beg from his mother and from his Bonaparte
relations. He plunged into politics, and even considered for a while standing as a candidate for the

position of President of the Second Republic in
opposition to Louis Napoleon. He induced the
latter to give him a small pension; he made all
manner of claims upon the Government, and
squandered whatever he obtained in a wild fashion.
He issued all sorts of remarkable suggestions, not
one of them of the slightest value, on every conceivable subject, and he raised the most frightful clamour
when they were disregarded. There is no doubt
that he was mentally deranged. He died in 1881
without having accomplished a single noteworthy
action.

There is a faint doubt as to Léon's paternity, due
to his mother's way of living, but the doubts are
countered by his striking physical resemblance to the
Emperor. Napoleon himself certainly believed him
to be his own child; perhaps if he could have foreseen
the later career of the child in question he would have
been more chary of his acknowledgment. The
whole affair seems to be very much wrapped in doubt;
Napoleon evinced for young Léon not half the care
which he displayed for his other sons, while Léon's
birth (perhaps because it took place while Napoleon
was away in Poland) did not rouse nearly as much
interest as Walewski's three years later.

It has already been said that at the time of Léon's
birth Napoleon's attention was occupied by a new
mistress; it was this particular mistress who has been
elevated by some writers to the proud position of
being " the only woman Napoleon ever loved," and
who certainly held whatever affection the Emperor
was able to display for a longer period than any other
woman. To begin with, she was of a rank and class
far different from any of her predecessors, Josephine
not excepted, while secondly she was far fonder of
him than was any other woman. The circumstances
in which the two met were romantic. Napoleon had
just overturned the Prussian monarchy; he had

advanced like lightning from the Rhine to the
Niemen, and he burst at the head of the Grand Army
into Poland, where never before had a French army
appeared. The Poles were in ecstasy. They had
not the least doubt that their period of slavery was
ended, and that the young conqueror would once
more unchain the White Eagle. Deputations
thronged to meet him, and mobs gave him homage
in the villages. At the little town of Bronia, not
far from Warsaw, a lady was presented to him at
her earnest request, for she had braved all the terrors
of the hysterical mob in order to meet him. She
proved to be hardly more than a child, and dazzlingly
beautiful. Napoleon thanked her for her kindness,
and said that he was anxious to see her again. The
whole interview barely lasted a minute, for it was
imperative that Napoleon should press on to Warsaw,
but it made a deep impression on both of them.

Marie Laczinska was the daughter of one of the
old noble families of Poland, and she had recently
married Anastase Colonna de Walewice-Walewska.
Although Marie's family was noble, it was hardly
to be compared with that of her husband, for
Anastase was not only the head of a house in whose
veins ran the bluest blood of Poland, but he also
traced his descent to the Roman family of Colonna,
and through them his line ran back into the mists
of history beyond the Carolings and the Merovings
until one could trace its source among the patrician
families of republican Rome. He was rich, he was
famous, he held vast power. The only objections
to him as a husband were that he was seventy years
old and already had grandchildren who were older
than Marie. In the minds of Marie's guardians
such objections were trivial, and the young girl was
forced into marriage with the old noble, to play
the part of Abishag to Walewska's David. She
was not fated to endure this for long, because

L

Napoleon had not forgotten the meeting at Bronia, and sought her at all the fêtes at which he appeared in Warsaw. The secret could not be kept, and soon all Poland was aware that the great Emperor was in love with the Polish lady. The nationalist party heard the news with wild exultation, and Poniatowski, the hope of Poland, called upon her to sacrifice herself for her country. The other great nobles pressed her feverishly, and they contrived to persuade Walewska (who, naturally, was the only man who was ignorant of what was going on) to bring his wife to a ball which Poniatowski was giving in the Emperor's honour.

Marie came reluctantly. She was dressed as plainly as possible, in white satin without jewels, and, once in the ballroom, she kept herself as far in the background as she could. To no purpose, however. Napoleon, overjoyed, observed her as soon as she appeared, and immediately sent to her and requested her to dance with him. She refused. Duroc and Poniatowski remonstrated with her, but she remained adamant. Many other French officers had already noticed her dazzling beauty, her rich fair hair and the blueness of her eyes, and they swarmed round her. Napoleon watched the proceedings jealously from the other end of the room. As soon as any one of his officers appeared to have made any progress, he called to his Chief of Staff, and that particular officer was sent off post haste to carry a message somewhere out in the bleak countryside a hundred miles away. The situation verged on the impossible. Napoleon in desperation made a tour of the room, speaking to all the hundreds of women present merely in order to exchange half a dozen words with the one who was the cause of all this trouble. When at last he reached Madame Walewska the interview was unsatisfactory. She was as pale as death, and said nothing. He was vastly and unusually embarrassed. "White upon white is a mistake, Madame," he said, looking at her pale cheeks. Then—"This is not the sort of reception I expected after——" Then he passed on, and left the ballroom soon after.

That same evening she received a wild, urgent note from Napoleon. Others followed in rapid succession. Poniatowski and all the fiery patriots of Poland implored her to yield. Her blind husband, infatuated by this remarkable new popularity, bore her to reception after reception. A mercenary old aunt of hers, tampered with by Poniatowski, flung herself into the business as well, and offered herself as go-between. At last she received a letter from Napoleon hinting that he would restore Poland if she would yield. She yielded. Napoleon did not restore Poland.

For Poland's sake she had broken her marriage vows and violated all the dictates of her conscience. Napoleon, in return, temporized and compromised. He erected the Grand Duchy of Warsaw out of territory torn from Prussia, but the Grand Duchy was not autonomous, it was not called Poland, it was only one-third the size of the old land of the White Eagle. Poor Marie protested to the best of her ability, to be soothed by fair words from the Emperor. At Napoleon's request she left Poland after Tilsit, and came to Paris, where she lived in extreme retirement, visited by Napoleon as often as he could manage. Her gentleness and dislike of display must have been grateful to Napoleon after his other experiences, and he passed many happy hours with her. She was by his side during the maelstrom of the Essling campaign, and at Schönbrunn, the Palace of the Cæsars, she told him she was about to bear him a child. She did not realize then that from that selfsame palace Napoleon would summon, in a few months' time, a young girl who

would supplant her in his affections, and who would
also bear him a son, who, in place of being a nameless
bastard, would bear the title of King of Rome. She
went back to her dear Poland for the event, and at
Walewice, in May, 1810, Alexander-Florian-Joseph-
Colonna-Walewski was born.   On her return to
Paris Napoleon had married Marie Louise.

Napoleon softened the blow for her as well as he
could. He heaped wealth upon her; he gave her
town houses and country houses; the Imperial
officials were always at her òrders, and the Imperial
theatres were always open to her. Her son, young
Walewski, was made a Count of the Empire.
Perhaps this was some consolation to her. Perhaps—
seeing that it was her son's birth which had determined Napoleon to make a new marriage—not.
Napoleon even found time during the turmoil of
the Campaign of France to make additional arrangements in their favour, but by this time whatever
remained of the affair had long since burnt itself
out.

After the fall of the Empire, Marie Walewska
seems to have considered herself free. She paid a
mysterious visit to Napoleon at Elba in 1814,
accompanied by her little son, and she was present
at the Tuileries on Napoleon's arrival there during
the Hundred Days, but apparently on neither
occasion was the old relationship renewed. In
1816 she married a distant cousin of the Bonapartes,
a certain d'Ornano, a Colonel of the Guard, but she
was not destined long to enjoy her new happiness.
Marie de Walewska died in December, 1817.

Poor Marie! Her life was short, but it must
have been full of bitterness. Napoleon's affairs of
the heart (if they are even worthy of that name)
all seem inexpressibly harsh and matter-of-fact.
He seemed to have a kind of Midas touch in
these matters, whereby everything honourable and

romantic with which he came into contact turned, not into gold, but into lead. Various authors have tried to infuse into his association with Marie de Walewska some gleam of romance, some essence of the self-sacrificing spirit which is noticeable in the parallel deeds of other monarchs, but they have failed. Marie certainly seems at first to have believed him to be a hero, a knight without reproach as well as without fear, but as soon as she was disillusioned she resigned herself to an existence as drab as if she had been once more a septuagenarian's wife, and not the mistress of an Emperor. Contemporary Parisian society was almost entirely ignorant of her existence. She paid no calls, and she received none. The few appearances she made at Court were such as were only to be expected from a Polish lady of high rank. Napoleon could not keep her love for long, and, though she was faithful to him as long as the Empire endured, she obviously considered herself free as soon as Napoleon was sent to St. Helena. It was not the long-drawn, heroic romance some writers have endeavoured to make it appear; rather was it a brief burst of passion, and then—monotony.

The baby Count of the Empire whom she left behind enjoyed a distinguished career. In appearance he certainly resembled his great father, but his talents never seem to have risen above a mediocre standard. Alexander - Florian - Joseph - Colonna - Walewski was mainly educated in France, but he was a Pole by birth, and he fought for Poland at the age of twenty during the rising of 1830-31. When Poland fell once more before the might of Russia, he returned to France, became a Frenchman, and served in the French army. The revolution of 1848 brought Napoleon III. to the front, and the new Emperor, with his power based on the frail fabric of a legend, saw fit to surround himself with names which recalled to men's minds the old splendours of the First Empire. Walewski received honours in plenty; he was Ambassador to the most important Courts of Europe, a Senator, and a Minister of State. He wrote learnedly on various subjects. But all his glory was only a pale reflection of his father's and cousin's; he suffered eclipse after Sedan, and when he died, aged seventy-two, he had, after all, made very little mark in the world. He had not played the part of a Don John of Austria, or even of a Monmouth. De Morny quite outshone him.

With Napoleon's marriage to Marie Louise and association with Madame Walewska, his casual amorous adventures came to a more or less abrupt end. It has been suggested that this was on account of increasing age, but Napoleon was only in the early forties, and this cannot be the true reason. However, the explanation is just as simple. Napoleon was devoted to his new wife, and he was frightfully busy. From the summer of 1812, two years after his second marriage, he was almost continuously in the field. His exertions and worries thenceforward were sufficient to occupy even him, without any other complications. One likes to think of him turning with relief from the agonizing strain of ruling Europe to snatch a few quiet minutes in the placid peace surrounding Marie Louise and her child. That is all. He had no other mistress. At Elba he lived with his sister and mother, with no woman to share his inner life. Perhaps this was policy, for Napoleon was trying hard to induce Marie Louise to join him, and he would naturally be chary of doing anything which might annoy her—ignorant as he was of her unfaithfulness. This may be the explanation of the briefness of Madame Walewska's visit; she may have come intending to join him, and he may have sent her away again, but the fact that she was accompanied by her brother and other relations militates against this theory. Moreover, Marie was

THE KING OF ROME

already close friends with d'Ornano. After the Hundred Days Napoleon was sent to St. Helena, and once again no woman accompanied him. The manifold rumours about Madame de Montholon and others at St. Helena seem to have no foundation whatever in fact. Thus practically all Napoleon's illicit loves are confined to the decade 1800-10, while the last decade is entirely clear of them.

Thus far we have only treated of women who were Napoleon's mistresses; but considerable interest also attaches to a large number of women who, although members of the Imperial circle, never attained this dubious honour. Perhaps of these the one who attained the greatest heights (and who, incidentally, did least to deserve it) was Désirée Clary. She was the sister of the lady whom Joseph Bonaparte made his wife, and whose dowry of six thousand pounds was so welcome to the struggling family. Désirée's own dowry would have been of the same amount, and Joseph and various other Bonapartes tried to induce Napoleon to marry her. He seems to have dallied with the idea; indeed, it is frequently stated that a contract of betrothal was drawn up, but, however it was, Napoleon broke off the negotiations rather abruptly when he went to Paris in 1795. There is hardly any doubt that he had flirted with Désirée rather excessively, and that, after making a deep impression upon her, he had wounded her deeply by his precipitate abandonment. Subsequently he tried to make amends in much the same manner as he employed with his discarded mistresses—he tried to find her a husband to whom he could give substantial promotion. But Désirée was once more unlucky, for the man Napoleon sent to her, General Duphot, was murdered almost on her threshold while she was staying at Joseph Bonaparte's Embassy in Rome.

Eventually she was approached by Bernadotte, during Napoleon's absence in Egypt, and married him. Subsequently she declared that she had done this because Bernadotte was the only man who could injure Bonaparte, but she must have been far-sighted indeed if she could perceive the career which was awaiting Bernadotte. Moreau, and half a dozen other generals, such as Augereau, were more powerful than Bernadotte at the time. Désirée's statement was probably made in the light of subsequent events.

It was Bernadotte who gained most by the marriage. He acquired at one stroke a venomous, if inert, ally in his wife, an enthusiastic supporter in Joseph, his brother-in-law, and a sure refuge in case of trouble in Napoleon's dislike of a scandal in his family. From this time on, Désirée received distinction after distinction, and soon she was Son Altesse Serène la Maréchale Princesse de Ponte Corvo, sister of the Queen of Spain, and a leading figure in Imperial society. Then came the greatest distinction of all, and she found herself Princess Royal of Sweden. This last she found rather upsetting, for she discovered she was expected to leave her beloved Paris to live in the bleakness of the Stockholm palaces. She said, tearfully and truthfully, that she had thought at first that her new rank was merely a titular distinction, of the same class as her sovereignty of Ponte Corvo. She refused absolutely to leave France, and so Bernadotte went alone to Stockholm, thence to lead his Swedes against the Empire, while his wife stayed on in Paris. It certainly was an anomalous position, and some authors have said that Désirée acted as a spy on behalf of the Allies during the war of liberation. However, we can be quite sure that Napoleon, whatever tenderness he still felt towards her, would not have tolerated her sending news of any value to her husband; incidentally, it is obvious that a woman to whose mind Ponte Corvo, with its six thousand inhabitants, was in the same class as Sweden, with its millions, could not have been of much use as a spy.

After 1815, fate overtook her, and she was borne away to spend the rest of her life in the spartan splendour of the palace in the Staden. From that time forth she and her husband were a disappointed couple, distrusted and despised by all Europe, he with his eyes turned lingeringly towards the France whose crown he believed he had so nearly attained, she thinking longingly of the gaiety and careless freedom of the Paris she had left behind, which now hated her with true Parisian virulence.

Napoleon's sisters married before the plenitude of his power, and the matches they made were not as splendid as they might have been later; it was for his younger but much more distant connections that Napoleon was able to find husbands of royal rank. It is curious to notice the extraordinary marriages which were arranged while the Empire was at its height. A niece of Murat's, who had been brought up as the ragged and bare-footed daughter of a small farmer, married Prince Charles of Hohenzollern-Sigmaringen, and among her grandchildren and great-grandchildren at the present day are the King of Rumania, the King of the Belgians and the Queen of Portugal. Several of the petty princelings of Germany, with thirty generations of royal descent behind them, married obscure little Beauharnais and Taschers de la Pagerie. Eugène de Beauharnais and Berthier married princesses of Bavaria, and Jerome received as bride a daughter of the King of Würtemberg.

Eugène's marriage had caused a difficult situation, for Augusta of Bavaria was already affianced to the Hereditary Prince of Baden, heir apparent to

the reigning Grand Duke. Napoleon had caused
the marriage contract to be broken, but he was in
no way disconcerted; he straightway found a new
bride for the Hereditary Prince. He selected
Stéphanie de Beauharnais, a " thirty-second cousin "
of Josephine's. Stéphanie was the merest child,
who had had the most extraordinary upbringing.
Her parents were of a shiftless character, like
various other Beauharnais, and after the Revolution Stéphanie had been dependent on an English
peeress, Lady de Bathe, who had arranged with two
nuns from the suppressed houses to look after her.
As soon as Napoleon heard of her existence, he
summoned her to Court, and in accordance with his
pronounced ideas on family loyalty, made himself
responsible for her support. Next he announced
to her that he had secured her a royal husband.
Stéphanie immediately became a person of consequence, because as yet royal marriages were by no
means common in the Bonaparte family. Their
Imperial Highnesses, Napoleon's sisters, naturally
turned like tigresses upon the interloper, and reduced
the fifteen-year-old child to tears more than once in
the presence of the Court. This was more than
Napoleon could stand, and by a single decree he
gave the girl precedence over the whole Imperial
family save himself and Josephine. He wished to
keep the House of Baden as satisfied as possible.
With the same idea he gave Stéphanie a marvellous
trousseau, a dowry of sixty thousand pounds, and
jewels costing the same amount. Her wretched
father, who had returned from exile, received an
income of three thousand pounds a year and a lump
sum of two hundred thousand francs. He had done
nothing to earn it; he was merely the father of the
girl who was marrying an ally of the Emperor's.

The period was one of general rejoicing, for
Austerlitz had just been won, and French domination

over Europe seemed assured. The fêtes of the
marriage were of unexampled splendour; there were
illuminations; there were fireworks; and there were
balls without number, at one of which over two
thousand persons appeared. But behind all the
rejoicings there was a curious tragi-comedy being
played, for poor Stéphanie, married at sixteen to a
man she had never met, displayed a disconcerting
reluctance to complete all the accompanying for-
malities. Night after night she insisted on a girl
friend sharing her room with her. The Hereditary
Prince grew restive; the whole Court knew of the
deadlock, and were proportionately amused. But
international politics cannot wait on a girl's whim;
war clouds were appearing again across the Rhine;
Prussia seemed bent on war, and it was important
for Napoleon to be sure of Baden's friendship.
Napoleon admonished Stéphanie with all the severity
of which he was capable; he terrified the wretched
girl into passivity, and when at last the newly married
couple set off for Carlsruhe Baden's support of
France was assured.

But the unhappiness which awaited all Napoleon's
favourites dogged poor Stéphanie to her grave. The
House of Zaehringen hated her as an intruder; her
male children all died in infancy, and when in 1818
her husband died she found herself without any
established position in a hostile land. Hints have
not been lacking that Charles of Baden died through
poison administered by the Hochberg family (of
morganatic descent from an earlier Elector), which
ultimately obtained the throne. But the strangest
story is that concerning Kaspar Hauser. In 1828 a
young man was found wandering in the streets of
Nuremberg, who had never seen the sunlight, and
whose whole appearance seemed to indicate that he
had been shut up in a cellar all his life. He did not
long survive his freedom. Stéphanie jumped to the

conclusion that he was her second son, born in 1811, who was supposed to have died as an infant while she was seriously ill. Many people have agreed with her, and have supposed that he had been kidnapped by the Hochbergs to prevent his inheritance of the throne. Some people go further, and boldly declare that after his escape he was poisoned. The whole matter has an aura of peculiarity, and it has attracted the attention of many writers of authority, among them Mr. Baring Gould. The most obvious counter to the theory that Kaspar Hauser was a son of Stéphanie is that the people who would be bold enough to kidnap him would have had the sense to kill him outright, and not to keep him as living evidence of their guilt. If they murdered him in 1828, they would certainly not have flinched from murdering him in 1811.

But Stéphanie always believed that Kaspar was her son, and she passed the last thirty years of her life in mourning a murdered husband, a murdered son, a lost throne, and the utter ruin of her whole life.

This is only one more example of the blight which Napoleon left upon the lives of nearly everyone with whom he came into close contact. All the people who were indebted to him for their entire personal advancement lived to see the day when they paid for a few golden hours with the most utter regret and bitterness. The only ones who "lived happily ever after" were those who had always regarded him with suspicion, like Macdonald, or those of inferior mental calibre, like Marie Louise, whom a strange Providence seemed to take under its own special care.

So much for Napoleon's relations with women. Nowhere can one find the least trace of romance or self-sacrifice on his part, and it can safely be said that no woman ever loved him devotedly. Never could

Napoleon have said of any woman's beauty, as
Richard III. said,

> " Your beäuty, that did haunt me in my sleep
> To undertake the death of all the world
> So I might live one hour in your sweet bosom."

In men he could inspire the utmost self-devotion;
it seems hateful to think first of the Cuirassiers, a
living torrent of steel, pouring cheering to their
deaths at Wagram at his command, and then of his
vulgar deceit of Walewska and his petty, mercenary
intrigues with other women.   It leaves a foul blot on
the splendour which surrounds him.

> " Methought I saw a slug crawl slavering
> Over the delicate petals of a flower."

CHAPTER XIV

LIKES AND DISLIKES

PERHAPS now we can see a little more clearly the man who was the centre of so much interest. To appreciate a man's character it is not so much necessary to realize what he did, as to realize what he wanted to do, what he was fond of doing, and what he would have done had he been able; and on the other hand it is equally necessary to realize what it was he did not like doing. With Napoleon these matters do not bear a great deal of analysis.

One is astonished at first when it is borne in upon one that Napoleon was a man of tepid desires in most directions. It seems almost inconceivable that the man who was the storm centre of Europe, who was capable of rousing overwhelming emotion in others, was nearly incapable of emotion himself. Yet so it was. Napoleon had one ruling desire—for work, and he had one ruling passion—for the army. His secondary passions were small, and his dislikes were equally small. Compared in this light to any full-blooded personality, Dr. Johnson, for instance, Napoleon fades away into dismal uninterestingness. Work was what Napoleon liked best of all in this world. When other men would have broken down under the simultaneous strain of work and anxiety, he throve and grew fat. One of his most famous letters was written on this very subject to his brother Joseph at the height of the Eylau campaign.

Joseph, from among the soft delights of Naples, had written complaining of the troubles which beset him while ruling his little kingdom, and Napoleon wrote back briefly and sternly, telling how he was at that moment engaged in a life and death struggle against Bennigsen; how he was encumbered with the difficulties of feeding and manœuvring two hundred thousand men in the boggy plains of Poland, where even he himself could hardly obtain the necessaries of life; how at the same time the affairs of half Europe demanded his attention, and yet for all this he did not allow himself to be worried by these numerous interests; he did all he had to do and delighted in the strain.

It can safely be said that Napoleon never took a holiday. Sometimes it has been hinted that in 1810 and 1811, after his marriage with Marie Louise, he slackened his pace and did not do as much as he might have done. This is true in part, but it is equally true that during that time he got through an amount of work which would have broken down most men. Napoleon was not made for holidays. It is hard to find, during the whole period covered by his correspondence, a single day in which he did not despatch a dozen letters, all of them bearing the hall-marks of the utmost care and thought, and nearly all of them vitally important links in a chain of important decisions. Inactivity was hateful to him. No sooner had he landed in Elba, removed entirely from the usual outlets of his energy, than he flung himself into the business of building up new interests. He laboured harder while governing his little island than did Kings of countries hundreds of times its size. Only when he was lodged in St. Helena, do we find a cessation of his frantic toil. Here circumstances were against him; his gaolers did their best in a blind fashion to prevent him from indulging in either mental or physical activity, while the climate and environments were both conducive to torpor. Yet even at St. Helena Napoleon was responsible for the production of a mass of written material of whose amount an average man might be proud if it were the results of the labour of a lifetime. Hard, unrelenting toil was to Napoleon the breath of life.

His chief relaxation was also in the nature of toil. Napoleon was passionately fond of all things military. Reviews were to him a source of unending delight. On emerging triumphant from a period of intense anxiety his first action almost invariably was to hold a review of all the troops he could muster; the very day on which he took up his residence at the Tuileries after the *coup d'état* of Brumaire, he reviewed on the Caroussel those battalions which later formed the nucleus of the Guard, while at Tilsit he contrived to arrange for two or three reviews every day. All the pageantry and pomp of war appealed irresistibly to this man to whom so little else appealed. To Napoleon a battalion marching past in column of double companies was worth all the vigour of Schiller and all the passion of Alfieri. Soldiers are a delight to most of us from our nursery days to our maturity; the sight of a long line of bayonets or the brilliance and glitter of the plumes and armour of the Household Cavalry can still make us catch our breath for an instant, but in few instances does this passion become overwhelming. When it becomes characteristic of a nation it usually portends calamity. Frederick William I. of Prussia suffered from it to an extent which has become historic, but in his case his passion for soldiers was so overwhelming that he did not risk losing any of his Potsdam Guards. Napoleon was different; he intended his army for fighting, and fight it did for twenty years, pomp and pageantry notwithstanding. Not the wildest calumniator has ever hinted that the reason why Napoleon did not send the Guard into action at Borodino was because

he wanted to keep them to review in peace-time—
though this explanation is sounder than some of those
put forward. Napoleon indulged his passion whenever possible, but he kept it nevertheless strictly
within bounds.

Napoleon had been a soldier from the age of
twelve, so that one can easily explain his liking for
military detail; he had been human from the day of
his birth, but it is not so easy to find any other human
traits or weaknesses. The pleasures of the table
meant nothing to him; twenty minutes sufficed for
dinner at the Tuileries, and he dined just as con-
tentedly on horse-steak in Russia as he did on the
elaborate dishes which delighted Marie Louise. So
far as can be ascertained Napoleon was never seen
drunk, or sea-sick, or dyspeptic. It would be almost
with relief that we would read of his suffering from
measles, had he ever done so. His freedom from
ordinary weaknesses tends to throw the whole picture
out of perspective. One can hardly be surprised that
even so sensible a man as Thiers lost his head while
telling of Napoleon's exploits. There is only one
human touch to which we can turn to gain the
measure of the whole. Napoleon loved a lord.

We have already described how ardently Napoleon
looked forward to his meeting with his Imperial
bride, and the complacency with which he referred to
her royal uncle and aunt his predecessors, Louis XVI.
and Marie Antoinette. The same characteristic is
noticeable in many of his actions. Perhaps it is
going to extremes to describe his origination of the
Legend of Honour as a piece of snobbery, but his
other arrangements for the provision of a titled
nobility are strongly indicative of this curious stray
littleness of mind. No one reading his letters can
doubt that he preferred speaking of Monsieur le
Maréchal Prince d'Essling, Duc de Rivoli, Grand
Aigle de la Légion d'Honneur to speaking of plain

M

General Masséna. He delighted in seeing about
him Grand Constables, Arch-Chancellors, Grand
Chamberlains; it pleased him to walk midst Grand
Dukes and Princesses; he preferred conversation
with the not over-talented Queen of Prussia to
any interview with Goethe. Characteristically, he
once invited an actor to come and perform before
a " Parterre of Kings." It may perhaps be pleaded
that his painstaking care in the regulation of precedence, and his minute examination of forms and
ceremonies were due to his desire to have his Imperial
arrangements perfect, but it may be pleaded with
equal justice that he entered voluntarily into these
arrangements. The Imperial dignity was not forced
upon him; he lost as many adherents by his assump-
tion of it as he gained. For all this, once Napoleon
decided upon indulging his snobbery, he indulged in
such a manner as to gain most profit by it. Just as
his delight in military matters tended towards the
improvement of his army, so his snobbery tended
towards buttressing his throne. Napoleon took
advantage of his own weaknesses just as he did of
other people's.

One searches in vain for other prominent
characteristics. The selfishness so often attributed
to him is not so much the selfishness of Napoleon as
the selfishness of the Emperor. One cannot call
selfish the young lieutenant who took upon himself
the maintenance of a brother when his sole income
was thirty pounds a year, nor the man who gave
crowns and fiefs and fortunes to his friends, but the
Emperor who pried jealously into the management
of his subject kingdoms and took them back if he
saw fit, the Emperor who refused to share his
glory with his general, the Emperor who sacrificed
thousands of lives in order to hold down Europe was
selfish because he believed the Imperial power would
suffer were he unselfish. Even the ambition with

which he is usually credited does not appear on close examination to be very remarkable or extraordinary. Ambition is, after all, one of the commonest of human traits, and varies only in degree and not in occurrence. When Napoleon was a young man he wanted to " get on " ; he " got on " partly through abundance of opportunity and partly through his extraordinary talent. If it be said that he succeeded through the force of his ambition, it can easily be countered that most of the men who have ever succeeded were ambitious. A quite plausible life of Napoleon might be written showing that he was entirely the reverse of ambitious, and that all the steps of his career towards power from the day of his receiving the command of the army of Italy to his invasion of Russia in 1812, were forced upon him. At the beginning of his career Napoleon had far less chance of gaining supreme power than had Hoche, or Pichegru, or Jourdan, or Moreau, but his rivals dropped out of the race through early deaths, sheer folly, or, perhaps in the case of Moreau, mere inertia. Napoleon is believed to have schemed to seize the reins of government as early as 1797, but half a dozen others, including even Bernadotte and Augereau, did the same. Napoleon was lucky, vigorous, and far more gifted than they, and it was into his hands that the ripened fruit dropped. From 1799 on, from the Consulate to the Consulate for life, from the Consulate for life to the Empire of the French, from the Empire of the French to the visionary Empire of the West, were steps. which he could hardly have avoided taking in some form or other if he wished to retain any power at all. The attempt to enforce the Continental System undoubtedly led him further forward than was wise or than he desired. Had Bonaparte been a Washington, he might have retired after the peace of Amiens, but it is perfectly possible that even if a series of Washingtons had succeeded

him, the last of them would have been beaten in a
great battle some ten years later by the armies of an
alliance of nations which had for some time back been
oppressed and enslaved in increasing degree by the
French. Undoubtedly this train of reasoning is
forced and unsound in some respects, but it certainly
gives a great deal of plausibility to the theory that
Napoleon's ambition was not so far-reaching and
impossibly aspiring as it is sometimes carelessly said
to have been. In addition, it is necessary to
remember that his restless energy must occasionally
have spurred him to further action while a lazier man
would have remained tranquil. This is possibly an
explanation of his suicidal plunge into Spanish affairs.

In like fashion the other indications of Napoleon's
character are faint and colourless. Women had no
vast attraction for him; he appreciated them as a
physical necessity, but that was all. Undoubtedly
he ranked women in his mind along with exercise and
medicine, as things without which men are liable to
deteriorate. Wit and humour had very little mean-
ing for him—as witness his distaste for Molière—
and Art had even less. He ransacked Europe to fill
the Louvre with masterpieces, but he himself did not
enjoy them. He was careless of his ease, of his
attire, of his comfort. When he fell from power, he
did not seem to resent it very much. There is a story
of his having attempted suicide after his abdication
in 1814, but it is much to be doubted. The details
seem far more in agreement with the symptoms of
his mysterious illness, or of the malignant disease of
which he died a few years later. He did not seem
vastly depressed at Elba, or even at St. Helena.
Comparable to this lack of depression is his hopeful-
ness during the hopeless campaign of 1814. He
stood to lose so much, and he lost so much, but
neither the possibility nor the loss weighed upon him
unbearably. Perhaps he was confident that more

PAULINE BORGHESE
(née BONAPARTE)

greatness awaited him in the future; perhaps he simply did not care. The furious rages in which Napoleon sometimes indulged seem to have been merely good acting; he himself admitted that he never allowed his rage to mount higher than his chin.

Another human trait which was wanting in Napoleon was the capacity for hatred. With his Corsican upbringing one might have expected to find him at feud with numbers of people, but he was not. Napoleon was not a good hater. He never hated Pozzo di Borgo, for instance, half as much as Pozzo hated him. He took violent dislikes to a few individuals, but he frequently overcame these in course of time. Macdonald is a case in point. Hating must be distinguished from despising. Napoleon despised the Spanish and Neapolitan Bourbons, but he did not hate them. He waged war after war on Francis of Austria, but he never admitted any personal dislike. Hatred and affection were alike unknown to Napoleon.

There are one or two isolated examples of men for whom Napoleon professed affection, but a good deal of doubt surrounds the matter. Napoleon said he was fond of Muiron, who gave up his life for him at Arcola; he said he was fond of Duroc, the Grand Marshal of the Palace, who was killed at Bautzen, but it is significant that we do not hear much about this affection in either case until after Duroc and Muiron were both dead. More than one contemporary writer, indeed, has hinted that Duroc disliked Napoleon, although he did his duty in an exemplary manner, while so little is known about Muiron that we can be permitted to assume that the affection Napoleon expressed after Duroc and he were dead was a theatrical touch assumed for the purpose of enlisting still more sympathy at St. Helena. This is quite in accordance with what we know both of

Napoleon's own nature and of his plan of campaign while in exile.

One more point.   Napoleon habitually attributed the lowest possible motives to all human actions. His attitude was not so much cynical as uncomprehending (though some people think that cynicism is merely lack of comprehension); he simply could not understand anyone making any self-sacrifice when quite disinterested or altruistic.   If anyone did, he put it down to hysteria.   The brave boys who died for him in the filth and misery of twenty campaigns were so enthusiastic, Napoleon thought, merely because they were hysterical.

This idea is plainly to be discerned on reading Napoleon's bulletins and proclamations.   They are all of them apparently designed to appeal to a sentimental and hysterical public.   Without doubt, they did appeal to their readers, but one cannot help feeling nowadays a sensation of distaste when looking through them.   They are unbearably reminiscent of street corner oratory and of the flamboyant efforts of the sensational press—appeals to hysteria pure and simple. Moreover, it is also plain that Napoleon himself felt none of these hysterical impulses—he was merely working cold-bloodedly on the passions of a passionate people.   Napoleon was entirely unfamiliar with noble instincts or with the idea of devotion.   He laid claim to them himself, of course, despite his disbelief in them, but that was merely another method of capturing the favour of the populace.   Washington's loftiness of character was as much a sealed book to him as would have been (had he lived to see it) Garibaldi's disinterested patriotism.

Even the sympathy with nationalism which his nephew later laboured so hard to attribute to him was wanting; the man who could unite seven nationalities into one state, and who tossed fragments of territory from one power to another without consulting anything beyond his own desires must of necessity have cared nothing either for national or individual sentiment.

We can sum up then by describing Napoleon as the embodiment of enormous ability, unquenchable energy, and—nothing else. He can be compared to an unguarded store of high explosive; he was bound to cause trouble wherever he settled. Once afforded an opportunity he was certain to bring about unexpected results, and, as it happened, the turmoil into which France was flung just as he reached manhood afforded a very early opportunity. Without morals or ideals to restrain or guide him, he would cause destruction wherever he went, like a runaway horse or a motor lorry out of control. He was a Frankenstein monster let loose on the world: the good he did was as haphazard as the harm.

CHAPTER XV

WHAT MIGHT HAVE BEEN

OFTEN and often it has been savagely pointed out that Napoleon enjoyed greater good fortune than anyone could with reason expect. Every incident in Napoleon's life, from his employment by Barras in 1795 to the collapse of Francis I.'s nerve in 1809, has been used to prove this, while his later misfortunes have been casually mentioned as being inevitable considering his careless taking of risks. The former criticism is undoubtedly fair, but the latter is open to serious disagreement, and has hardly received the opposition it deserves.

Napoleon's domination of Europe from 1805 onwards depended entirely upon his military supremacy; nobody would dream of saying that he would have received the homage of the Confederation of the Rhine, the submission of Prussia and the co-operation of Austria simply because of the force of his personality, if that personality had not also been supported by the menace of four hundred battalions. Consequently Napoleon's policy could not be questioned so long as his army was invincible, and mistakes of policy could be rapidly erased by a victory in the field. Similarly a military error was of far more importance than a political one; if the Bonapartes had never met with a defeat in battle their line would still inevitably hold the throne of

France, with a ring of subject countries round them. It is therefore of the first importance to inquire into the failure of the army; the other failures are merely secondary. Thus if anyone says that he has just quitted a certain building for three reasons, one of them being that he was thrown out, the other two reasons are of secondary importance.

Various dates have been assigned to the commencement of the decline of Napoleon's military ascendancy, and the very fact that this is so proves how difficult it is to be dogmatic on the subject. Napoleon lost battles in 1807, and he won battles in 1813—and 1814 and 1815 for the matter of that. The quality of the material at his disposal certainly grew more and more inferior as time went on, but it is easy to make too much of this point, for Napoleon was *never* defeated except by superior numbers. However, the first time he met with serious disaster was, undoubtedly, in the campaign of 1812. The catastrophe has been described times without number; what has not so often been mentioned is the nearness of Napoleon's approach to another triumph.

A Napoleonic army never took the field without the full expectation of losing half its numbers through hardship, as distinct from the action of the enemy. This was the price it paid for its rapidity of marching and its freedom from a rigid dependence upon its base. If Napoleon led half a million men to attack Russia, he expected to lose a quarter of a million before he was in a position to gain a decisive success; he certainly lost the quarter million, and he certainly gained a success, but the losses continued and the success was not decisive. And yet on several occasions it appeared as if a new Austerlitz or a new Friedland were at hand.

The irony of the situation lies in the fact that in 1812 Napoleon took much more extensive measures

to ensure that losses due to poverty of supplies would
be minimized than he did in any other campaign.
He organized an elaborate Intendance, with vast
trains of wagons, and he collected enormous depôts
of stores wherever possible.   The system broke down
almost at once, partly on account of the inexperience
of the commissariat staff, partly because of torrential
rains which ruined the roads as soon as the army
started, and partly because the army and train were
so huge that they had already absorbed every available horse in Europe, so that losses (which necessarily
increased with the distance marched from the depôts)
could not be replaced at all.   This threw additional
work on the surviving horses, thereby increasing the
wastage, so that the Intendance went to pieces at a
rate increasing by geometrical progression.   Before
very long the Grand Army was once more dependent
entirely on the country through which it marched,
and the numbers were vast and Lithuania and White
Russia were miserably poor.   It was a combination
of circumstances apparently almost justifying the
Russian boast that God was on their side.

Yet matters were not progressing any too well
for the Russians.   Their field army was hopelessly
divided ; one portion, from the Danube, could not be
expected for months, while of the other two parts
one was almost in the clutches of the French, and
the two together were hopelessly inferior in numbers
to the forces at Napoleon's disposal.   The tide of
war came surging back across Russia ; the Russians
were marching desperately to escape from the trap ;
the French were pursuing equally desperately in the
hope of closing the last avenue of escape.   The
balance wavered, but at length turned in favour of
the Czar.   The roads were mere mud tracks, churned
by the Russians into quagmires, and the French were
delayed.   Jerome Bonaparte was not as insistent on
speed as he might have been, and at last, after fierce

rearguard fighting, Bagration escaped from the snare laid for him. A little more—ever so little!—and Smolensk might have been another Ulm.

The two main Russian armies were now combined, and, a hundred and twenty thousand strong, with a numerous cavalry, they were able to sweep the country bare before the French advance. Had the French movements round Smolensk been successful, the Russians would have had only half these numbers, and they would probably have been panic-stricken in addition; the French advance would have been proportionately easier and less expensive. In fact, it is difficult to see how Russia could have continued the war, for Alexander's nerve would have been shaken, the war party would have received a severe rebuff, and altogether an entirely different atmosphere would have arisen. The Russians fell slowly back towards Moscow, the French, starving and disease-ridden, toiled painfully after them. Barclay de Tolly was relieved from his command in consequence of his inaction, and Kutusoff, the disciple of the great Suvaroff, took his place. A battle was fought at Borodino. For Napoleon, it was the first victory which did not give him huge captures of prisoners and the prompt and abject submission of his enemies; for the Russians it seemed as good as a victory, for they had met the great conqueror *en rase campagne*, and had escaped.

Yet they should not have done. The late Lord Wolseley declares that Napoleon's plan of attack at Borodino " could not be more perfectly conceived or better elaborated," and he goes on to say that it was a sudden attack of illness which prevented Napoleon from controlling the battle when it reached its height, and from sending adequate supports to Ney at the crucial moment. This is the first mention we find of the mysterious illness on which a large number of writers lay so much stress; in the next campaign we

shall find a much more important example. But
whether Napoleon was ill or not, a little better
luck for Ney or Davout would certainly have
brought about important results. The destruction
of Kutusoff's army would have had a great effect
on the rest of the campaign, even if it had not
appalled Alexander into making peace.

The next mistake of the Emperor's was in staying
too long at Moscow; during the five weeks he spent
there his own army became demoralized, the Russians
had time to rally and to bring up the Army of the
Danube, and winter closed down on the countryside.
When at last Napoleon decided to retreat Kutusoff
was able at Malo-Jaroslavetz to bar the way to
Kaluga, and to force him to go back through the
pillaged districts through which he had come; this
could mean nothing less than the destruction of his
army, and, as everyone knows, the Grand Army was
destroyed. It is needless here to tell once more the
tale of the Beresina and Krasnoi; the interest of
" what might have been " ceases with the battle of
Malo-Jaroslavetz.

The points to be remembered are that during the
fighting round Smolensk Napoleon was within a hairbreadth of an overwhelming victory; at Borodino he
might have gained a satisfactory victory; a prompt
retreat from Moscow would at least have minimized
disaster; a success at Malo-Jaroslavetz would have
saved part of the army, while the check which was
actually experienced here was due to the accumulated
effects of the earlier bad luck. In a military sense
the campaign of 1812 was not merely justifiable but
it was very nearly justified. A little—a very little
more thrown into the scale would have saved his
Empire for Napoleon and set him on a higher throne
than ever before.

The campaign of 1813 was in this sense even
more striking. It was waged with untrained,

immature forces, for the most part against overwhelming odds, but during the course of the fighting
Napoleon was not once, but many times, within an
ace of successes more splendid than Austerlitz. The
actions of the Allies seemed to portend failure for
them from the start. Although Prussia joined
Russia as soon as the extent of the French disaster
became known; although there was nothing to bar
their way except a few thousand starving survivors
of the Grand Army; although all Germany was
in a ferment, and the French domination of the
Rhenish Confederation was tottering, the Russians
advanced with pitiful caution and delay. Napoleon
had returned to Paris, had raised, organized, equipped
and set in motion a new army of a quarter of a
million men by the time the Russians reached the
Elbe. Almost before the Russian commander-in-
chief, Wittgenstein, knew what was happening,
Napoleon had rushed back at the head of his new
army, had won the battle of Lützen, had reconquered
Saxony, and had flung the Allied army back across
the Oder.

At Bautzen they stood once more to fight.
Napoleon drew up the most gigantic battle plan ever
conceived up to that time; with half his force he
assailed the Allied centre, while Ney with sixty
thousand men marched against the right. The
struggle lasted for twelve bitter hours. Somehow
Napoleon held his own command together and
kept the Allies pinned to their position, while Ney
was slowly wheeling his immense force round for
the decisive movement. But the stars in their
courses fought against the Emperor. Ney failed
lamentably. He lost sight of the main object of his
march, and he showed his hand and then wasted his
strength in a fierce attack on Blücher at Preistitz.
Blücher struggled gamely; more and more of Ney's
forces were drawn into the fight; the turning move-

ment was delayed, and the Allies, warned in time, writhed out of the trap. Fifty thousand prisoners and two hundred guns might have been captured; as it was, Napoleon was left to deplore a massacre—for nothing! Alluding to Soult's capture of Badajoz in 1811, Napoleon had said, "Soult gained me a town and lost me a kingdom." He might well have said of Ney's attack on Preistitz that Ney gained him a village and lost him an Empire. It is inconceivable that the war could have been prolonged if Ney had obeyed orders at Bautzen; the allied army comprised all the troops that Russia and Prussia could at that time put into the field; its destruction would have meant the reconquest of Prussia and of Poland, the intimidation of Austria, and the regaining of Napoleon's European ascendancy.

After Bautzen Napoleon concluded an armistice with his enemies. He still hoped for an advantageous peace, and even if he failed to obtain this he expected that the delay would enable him to rest the weary boys who filled the ranks, to drill his wretched cavalry into some semblance of order, and to clear his rear of the bandits and partisans who were swarming everywhere. Moreover, for the last eighteen months he had been working at a pace which would have killed most men, and he himself was undoubtedly feeling the strain. The armistice would give him a little rest. But it meant disaster, nevertheless. From all over Russia new recruits were plodding across the unending plains to fill the gaps in the ranks of the field army; Prussia was calling out her whole male population, and Bernadotte's Swedes were gradually moving up into line. Worse than all, Austria turned against him. The delay enabled Francis to bring his army up to war strength on the receipt of lavish English subsidies, and, even while he still hesitated to attack his son-in-law, the news arrived that Wellington had routed

Joseph Bonaparte at Vittoria, had cleared Spain of the French, and was about to attack the sacred soil of France herself. The news was decisive, and the demands of the Allies promptly increased inordinately. When, in August, the armistice came to an end, Napoleon found himself assailed by forces of twice his strength.

Yet he did not despair; he thrust fiercely into Silesia, and then, finding the Austrians moving against Dresden, he wheeled about, marched a hundred and twenty miles in four days, and gained at Dresden the most surprising of all his victories. With a hundred thousand men he flung back a hundred and sixty thousand Russians and Austrians in utter disorder; Vandamme had cut off their retreat, and once again it seemed as if Ulm and Austerlitz were to be repeated. And then once more occurred a startling change of fortune. Napoleon might have taken a hundred thousand prisoners; the Emperors of Austria and of Russia might have fallen into his power; Austria would have been ruined, and Napoleon could have dictated peace on his own terms. But Napoleon handed over the pursuit to Murat and St. Cyr, and returned to Dresden. In consequence, the retreating Austrians were not pressed, Vandamme was overwhelmed, and the action at Kulm gave the Allies twenty thousand prisoners instead of placing the whole Allied army in the hands of the French.

No one knows why Napoleon returned to Dresden when victory was in his grasp. The advocates of the illness theory certainly have a strong case here; but perhaps it was news of the disasters in Silesia which recalled him; perhaps he was merely too tired to continue; perhaps he only had a bad cold as the result of sitting his horse all day in the pelting rain which fell all day during the battle of Dresden. However it was, Napoleon's

mastership of Europe was lost irreparably when he
came to his decision to leave his army.

For two months disaster now followed disaster.
Macdonald had already been routed on the Katzbach;
Oudinot was beaten at Gross Beeren, Ney was beaten
at Dennewitz, St. Cyr surrendered at Dresden, and
Napoleon himself tasted the bitter cup of defeat at
Leipzig.   The astonishing feature of the autumn
campaign of 1813 was not that Napoleon was
defeated, but that he ever escaped from Germany
at all.   But he did, blotting out on his path the
Bavarian army which opposed him at Hanau.

Once again the Allies advanced too slowly, and
once again Napoleon was able to organize a fresh
army to defend France.   Soult had grappled with
Wellington in the south, and was stubbornly con-
testing every inch of French soil in his desperate
campaign of Toulouse.   Napoleon prepared to make
one more effort for success in the north.   Russia,
Austria, Prussia, Sweden, the Confederation of the
Rhine, Holland and even Belgium had sent every
man available against him.   Four hundred thousand
men were about to pass the Rhine while Napoleon
had not a quarter of this force with which to oppose
them.   However, the prospect was not as hopeless
as it would appear.   The Allies were bitterly jealous
of each other, and Napoleon had good grounds for
hoping to divide them even now.   Besides, they were
all of them intent upon gaining possession of whatever
territory they wished to claim at the conclusion of
peace, and an army guided solely by political motives
is at the mercy of another which is directed only in
accordance with the dictates of military strategy.

This early became obvious.   Austria had bought
the alliance of the smaller German states only by
means of extensive guarantees of their possessions;
in consequence she determined to find compensation
for her losses by acquisitions in Italy.   But Italy

was stoutly defended by the Viceroy Eugène; she could make no progress there, and in consequence she did not yet desire Napoleon's fall. Schwartzenberg, the Austrian general, was therefore held back by Metternich's secret orders until Venetia and Lombardy should be in Austrian hands. Metternich was quite capable of leaving the Russians and Prussians in the lurch while he played his own tortuous game; however, the situation was saved by Murat's betrayal of Napoleon. With Murat on his side, and the Neapolitan army moving forward against Eugène, Metternich was sure of Italy, and Schwartzenberg was allowed to proceed into France. Once more the weakness and treachery of a subordinate had prevented Napoleon from gaining a decisive success.

The prospect grew gloomier and gloomier for the French. Napoleon was beaten at Brienne and at La Rothière; immediate and utter ruin seemed inevitable. Suddenly everything was changed. Napoleon fell upon the dispersed army of the Allies. At Champ-Aubert, Vauchamp, Château-Thierry and Mormant the Allies were beaten and hurled back. More than this, the Prussians under Blücher, thirty thousand strong, hard pressed by Napoleon, came reeling back towards Soissons and the Marne—and Soissons was held by a French garrison. With an unfordable river before him; the only bridge held by the enemy; a panic-stricken army under his command, and Napoleon and his unbeaten Frenchmen, flushed with victory, at his heels, Blücher seemed doomed to destruction. The officer in command at Soissons bore the ominous name of Moreau; he was intimidated into surrender when one more day's defence would have had incalculable results. Blücher escaped across the Marne not a minute too soon.

This was Napoleon's last chance before his
N

abdication.   His armies were weakened even by their
victories; the Allied forces seemed inexhaustible.
All Napoleon's efforts were unavailing; his final
threat at Schwartzenberg's communications was
disregarded, and the Allies reached Paris.   Marmont's surrender here has often been brought
forward as one more instance of treachery in high
places, but it was not treachery, it was only timidity
and fear of responsibility.   One cannot imagine
Blücher surrendering under similar circumstances.
Be that as it may, Paris fell, and Napoleon abdicated.

After the abdication came the descent from
Elba; after the descent from Elba came the Hundred
Days; and at the end of the Hundred Days came the
Waterloo campaign.   It was during the Waterloo
campaign that there occurred, not one but half a
dozen chances for Napoleon to win the decisive
victory for which he had been striving ever since
1812, but all these half-dozen chances were spoilt
by unexpected happenings and by sheer hard luck.

Many critics have inveighed against Napoleon's
decision to take the initiative into his own hands
and to carry the war into the enemy's camp by
his invasion of Belgium, but there is hardly one
who can find any fault with the plan of invasion
once it had been decided upon.   The chief fault-
finder, indeed, is Wellington, who, to his dying
day, maintained that the movement should have
been commenced through Mons, against the English
right, and not through Charleroi, against their left.
However, Wellington's opinion on this matter does
not carry as much weight as it might, because the
Iron Duke was guilty of several serious mistakes
during the campaign, and was only too anxious to
draw any red herring that offered across their trail,
especially as these mistakes were nearly all committed
while he was under the impression that Napoleon's
ultimate objective was his right and not his centre.

The whole weight of later opinion is in favour of Napoleon's plan.

Napoleon decided, then, to invade Belgium via Charleroi, to interpose between the Prussian and the Anglo-Allied armies and defeat them in detail. The fact that he had only 130,000 men against 120,000 Prussians and 100,000 English and Allies does not seem to have caused him any grave apprehension. The greatest handicap under which he suffered was the absence of Berthier and Davout; both staff work and the higher commands suffered because of this, for Soult had no aptitude for the task of Chief of Staff, and Ney and Grouchy had no skill either in higher strategy or in the handling of large numbers of men. Nevertheless, the initial movements, without the interference of the enemy, were carried out with brilliant success; the 130,000 men available were assembled on the Sambre without either Blücher or Wellington having any suspicion as to the storm that was gathering. Next day the advance across the Sambre was ordered, and the storm burst.

The two vitally important factors for success were extreme simplicity of movement and the utmost secrecy of design. But these were rendered impossible at the very moment of the opening of the campaign. First, a general of division, as soon as he was over the river, deserted to the Prussians and disclosed the very considerable information of which he was possessed, and secondly the officer bearing orders to Vandamme to advance met with an accident and broke his leg. This held up both Vandamme's corps and the one behind it, Lobau's, and delayed the advance after the movement had become known for six valuable hours. All chance of surprising the Prussians in their cantonments was now lost, but for all that the plan of campaign was so perfect that on the next day the English and Prussians could only

bring slightly superior numbers to bear on the French
force.   At Ligny the Prussians were beaten; at
Quatre Bras the English were held back.   Ney's
and d'Erlon's mistakes on this day have already
been described.   Had Ney acted with all possible
diligence, or had d'Erlon used his wits, either a
completely crushing victory over the Prussians or a
nearly equally satisfactory success over the English
could have been obtained.   Even both were possible.
But Napoleon's chance was spoiled owing to the
inefficiency of his subordinates.   Soult, Ney and
d'Erlon were all equally to blame.

The next point is more mysterious.   After Ligny
was fought and won, it was clearly to Napoleon's
advantage to follow up his success without a moment's
delay.   No other general had ever been so remorseless in hunting down a beaten enemy, and in wringing
every possible advantage from his victory.   But at
Digny Napoleon paused.   No order for an advance
was issued.   For twelve hours paralysis descended
upon the Imperial army.   The Prussians struggled
out of harm's way, and crawled painfully by by-
roads to Wavre to keep in touch with the English.
The cavalry reconnaissances which were sent out
later the next morning to find the Prussian army
did their work badly, and left Napoleon convinced
that they had fallen back on Liège and not on
Wavre.   It was the delay, however, and not the
faulty scouting, which proved most disastrous.   Like
Napoleon's return to Dresden in 1813, it has never
been explained.   Some historians say that he was
struck down by an attack of the same nameless
illness which had overcome him at Borodino, at
Moscow, at Dresden and at Leipzig.   In this case
it is the only possible explanation.   For four or five
hours Napoleon must have suffered from a complete
lapse of his faculties.   Those four or five hours were
sufficient to ruin the Empire.   Napoleon was left

DAVOUT
(PRINCE D'ECKMÜHL AND DUC D'AUERSTÄDT)

completely in the dark as to the moral, strength and position of the Prussians, and consequently he detached Grouchy with ambiguous orders in pursuit, gave him a force too small for decisive operations and yet much too large for mere observation, and sent him by a route which precluded him either from assisting the main body or from interfering seriously with the operations of the Prussians.   Grouchy might possibly have done both if only he had possessed vast insight, vast skill and vast determination, but he did not; he was merely ordinary.   So Wellington turned to bay at Waterloo; the Prussians assailed Napoleon's flank, and the day ended in despair and disaster.

Thus, on looking back through the years of defeat, 1812, 1813, 1814 and 1815, we find that there were a great number of occasions when Napoleon might have gained a success which would have counter-balanced the previous reverses.   At Smolensk he might have gained another Friedland; at Borodino he might still have snatched some slight triumph out of the Moscow campaign.   At Bautzen he came within an ace of destroying the Russian and Prussian armies, at Dresden he nearly captured the whole Austrian army and the two most powerful autocrats of Europe.   The surrender of Soissons just saved the Prussians in 1814.   In 1815 he might have shattered either or both of the armies opposed to him. It is not too much to say that with the good luck which had attended him during his earlier campaigns not only might he not have been forced to abdicate in 1814, but he might have enjoyed his continental ascendancy for a very considerable additional length of time.

Beside these undoubted possibilities there are others not as firmly based.   Marbot tells a story that on the eve of Leipzig, while at the head of his Chasseurs, he saw a party of horsemen moving about in the darkness a short distance ahead. For various reasons he refrained from attacking—to discover later that the hostile force had consisted of the King of Prussia, the Emperors of Austria and Russia, and their staffs. A resolute charge by Marbot would have brought back as prisoners all the brains and authority of the opposing army. The Spanish victory at Pavia, when Francis the First lost " everything except honour," would have been a poor success in comparison. We have, however, only Marbot's word for this incident, and Marbot is distinctly untrustworthy. Edward III.'s army was not the only one which used the long bow.

It is more to the purpose to consider Dupont's surrender at Baylen. When Dupont was sent out from Madrid to conquer Andalusia, there was only one Spanish field army in being, and that was the one he was to attack. As it happened, his nerve failed him, he frittered away weeks of valuable time, and finally he was hemmed in and forced to surrender rather feebly. The news of the disaster spread like wildfire over the Peninsula. Moncey was repulsed from Valencia; Catalonia broke into insurrection and hemmed Duhesme into Barcelona. Galicia and Aragon began to arm. The Peninsular War was soon fully developed; it was to absorb the energies of an army of three hundred thousand men for five years; it was to shed the blood of half a million Frenchmen; it was to encourage first Austria, then Russia, to rebel against the Napoleonic domination, and it was only to end when the British flag waved over Bordeaux and Toulouse. Had Lannes or some other really capable officer been in command of Dupont's twenty thousand men, the Army of Andalusia might have been thoroughly beaten and the Peninsula overawed, for Baylen was the battle which destroyed the French army's reputation for invincibility. Had not the Spaniards been victorious there, there would not have been an opportunity for the simultaneous call to arms which set all Spain in an inextinguishable blaze; isolated outbreaks might naturally have occurred, but the long respite given to the Spaniards during the summer of 1808, while Madrid was evacuated, would not have taken place to give the Peninsula its opportunity for arming and organizing.   Baylen is as great a turning-point in Napoleonic history as even Bautzen or Leipzig— and but for Dupont history might have turned in another direction.

Instances such as this might be multiplied indefinitely, from Marmont at El Bodin (where he hesitated when half the British army was in his power) to Jourdan in his retreat to Vittoria; from Jerome's mismanagement of Westphalia to Ney at Dennewitz; but it is useless to continue.   It is obvious that Napoleon's military set-backs were due very largely, not to his own failings, but to the incapacity of his subordinates.   Napoleon made mistakes, enormous ones, sometimes (a few will be considered in the next chapter), but none of them as utterly fatal as those of the other generals.   And yet these other generals were quite good generals as far as generals go—they were far and away superior to Schwartzenberg and Wittgenstein, for instance. Only Wellington and perhaps Blücher can be compared to them.   The only moral to be drawn is that nothing human and fallible could sustain the vast Empire any longer; the dead weight of the whole was such that the least flaw in any of the pillars meant the progressive collapse of the entire fabric.

This conclusion enables us to approach a definite decision as to " what might have been."   It is unnecessary to argue as to whether the English Cabinet would have survived a defeat at Waterloo, or whether Francis would have made peace if he had been captured at Dresden.   The result eventually

would have been the same. There was only one
Napoleon, and the Empire was too big for him to
govern. Sooner or later something would go wrong,
and the disturbance would increase in geometrical
progression, and with a violence directly proportion-
ate to the length of time during which the repressive
force had been in action. It was inevitable that the
Empire should fall, although as it happened the fall
was accelerated by a series of unfortunate incidents.
Victor Hugo meant the same thing when he said
" God was bored with Napoleon "; and Napoleon
himself had occasional glimpses of the same inevitable
result—as witness the occasion when he said, " After
me, my son will be lucky if he has a few thousand
francs a year."

Thus, if Napoleon by good fortune had re-
established his Empire in 1813, and taken advantage
(just as he did in 1810) of peace in the east to
reconquer Spain in the south, even then he would
not long have retained his throne. The persistent
enmity of England would have continued to injure
him, and to seek out some weak spot for the decisive
blow. Even if Ferdinand had been sent back to
Spain, and French prestige survived such a reverse,
there would have still remained various avenues of
attack. England was suffering severely, but France
was suffering more. Perhaps the patience of the
French would have become exhausted, and some
trivial revolt in Paris would have driven Napoleon
into exile. A very similar thing happened in 1830,
and the house of Orleans was always anxiously
awaiting some such chance. There could hardly
have arisen a Napoleonic Legend in that event. To
the French mind Napoleon the Great and Napoleon
the Little would have been the same person, instead
of uncle and nephew.

However it was, Napoleon was not destined to
live long, and even if his Empire had survived him,

at his death one can hardly imagine Europe remaining under the thumb of any Council of Regency he might appoint, with Joseph and Jerome and the Murats all scheming and conspiring to grasp the main power. Poor silly Marie Louise could never have kept order; some Monk would have arisen to restore the Bourbons, and Napoleon II. would have received the same treatment as did Richard Cromwell. The legend of l'Aiglon would then have been very different. A Bonaparte restoration in France might be as feasible as ever was a Protectorate restoration in England. Not all Louis Napoleon's wiles could have built up a reactionary party; not all the glamour of Austerlitz and Jena could have masked the discredit of a new dynasty being cast out by its own people instead of by a league of indignant autocrats; even Sédan was not the death-blow to Bonapartism. As it is, there will be a Third Empire in France as soon as there arises a Napoleon the Fourth.

CHAPTER XVI

SPOTS IN THE SUN

IT was Napoleon's fate, during his lifetime and for some time after, to have his worst mistakes overlooked, and to have various strokes of policy violently condemned as shocking errors. Everyone has heard the execution of the Duc d'Enghien spoken of as " worse than a crime—it was a blunder." It is difficult to see why. Perhaps Fouché, to whom the remark is attributed, did not see why either. If a man should happen to think of an epigram of that brilliancy, it is hard to condemn him for using it without troubling much as to its truth. But whether launched in good faith or not, that shaft of wit sped most accurately to its mark, and proved so efficiently barbed that it has stuck ever since.

The real point was that France was at war with England at the time, and that Napoleon was so universally dreaded that any stick was considered good enough to beat him with. Consequently a storm of indignation arose, diligently fostered by those who benefited, and soon all Europe was furious that a poor dear Bourbon had been shot. If nowadays the President of the German Republic were to lay hold of a young Hohenzollern and shoot him on a charge of conspiracy, it is doubtful whether it would cause any similar stir. Europe is not fond of Hohenzollerns, and the principle of Legitimacy is so far discredited that it is not considered blasphemy to treat the descendant of an autocrat with violence.

Undoubtedly it was a crime for Napoleon to shoot the Duke, but it was hardly a blunder. It was contrary to international law for him to send the expedition to Ettenheim which arrested d'Enghien; it was contrary to statutory law to try him without allowing him to make any defence; it was contrary to moral law to shoot him for an offence of which he was not guilty. For all this Napoleon deserves the utmost possible censure—but without doubt he profited largely. Everywhere among Napoleon's enemies arose a weeping and wailing; the English poured out indignant seas of ink (in 1914 they wrote in much the same fashion about Wilhelm of Germany's withered arm). Alexander of Russia put his Court in mourning (only three years before he had been cognisant of the plot which brought about the murder of his own father); the King of Sweden tried to organize a crusade of revenge; but a month after d'Enghien died the Senate begged Napoleon to assume the Imperial title. It is curious, indeed, that so much notice should have been taken of one more murder by a generation which witnessed, without one quarter so much emotion, the partition of Poland, the storming of Praga, the sack of Badajoz, the shooting of Ney, and Wellington's devastation of the Tagus Valley. The art of propaganda was at quite a high level even more than a century ago.

Once again, the execution of d'Enghien was a crime and not a mistake. By it Napoleon showed that he was no mere Monk dallying with the idea of restoring the Bourbons. He brought to his support all the most determined of the irreconcilables. He showed the monarchs of Europe that he was a man to be reckoned with. Murat, Savary, everyone implicated was cut off from all possible communication with the Bourbons. The deed cowed the Pope into submission at a vitally important moment, while the mere mention of it later was sufficient to frighten

the wretched Ferdinand of Spain into abject obedience at that strange conference at Bayonne, when an
idiotic father and a craven son handed the crown of
Charles V. to an incompetent upstart.   But Napoleon
would have met with no more than he deserved had
he had dealt out to him at Fontainebleau in 1814 the
same tender mercy which Condé's heir received at
Vincennes ten years before—ten years almost to the
day.

If Enghien's execution were a crime but not a
mistake, there are several incidents, most of them
occurring about the same time, which undoubtedly
indicated mistakes, even if they were not crimes.
Thus Pichegru was found dead in prison.   Pichegru
was one of the generals of the Republic, almost
worthy of ranking with Hoch and Kléber.   He had
conquered Holland, and was credited with the
mythical exploit of capturing the frozen-in Dutch
fleet with a squadron of Hussars.   (The Dutch had
obligingly forestalled this achievement by surrendering some time previously.)   Later he had been found
to be parleying with the Bourbons, and had been
disgraced and exiled.   Returning at the time of
Cadoudal's conspiracy, he had been arrested,
imprisoned—and was found one morning dead, with
a handkerchief round his neck which had been
twisted tight by means of a stick.   Paris gossip
credited Napoleon with the guilt of his death, and
darkly hinted that his confidential Mamelukes had
revived the Oriental process of bowstringing.   It is
hard to believe that Napoleon really was guilty, for
he could have secured Pichegru's death by legal
methods had he wished, while if he wanted to kill
Pichegru quietly he could have adopted more subtle
means.   The blunder lay in his allowing the circumstances to become known; with his power he could
have arranged a much more satisfactory announcement which would leave no doubt in men's minds

that Pichegru really had committed suicide. In consequence of his carelessness Napoleon was also charged with the murder, a year later, of an English naval officer, Captain Wright, who also committed suicide in prison.

A more terrible mystery surrounds the death of Villeneuve. This unfortunate man had been in command at Trafalgar; he had been wounded and taken prisoner, and had subsequently been sent back to France. As soon as he landed he found that Napoleon was furious with him as a consequence of his defeat, and he was found dead in his room at Rennes, with half a dozen knife-stabs in his body. It was announced that he had committed suicide, but there are several unpleasant facts in connection with his death which point to another conclusion. Letters from him to his wife and from his wife to him had disappeared in the post; the manner of death was strange, for the knife-thrusts were numerous and one of them was so situated that it could hardly have been self-inflicted. Perhaps Napoleon had Villeneuve killed; perhaps the crime was committed by over-zealous underlings; however it was, it was a serious error on Napoleon's part to have allowed any room for gossip whatever. A possible motive for the crime (if it was one) lies in the fact that Napoleon was terribly anxious to keep secret the news of Trafalgar; not until the Restoration was the general French public acquainted with the fact that the French fleet had been destroyed—Napoleon had never admitted more than the loss of one or two ships.

It was incidents of this nature which caused the feeling of distrust which gradually arose in the minds of the French people. Broken treaties and international bad faith did not move them so much, partly because they were never in possession of the true facts, partly because a series of brilliant victories wiped off the smudges from the slate, and partly because international morality was at its usual low ebb; but tales of official murder and of unsavoury scandals in high places constitute the ideal food for gossip, and rumours spread and were distorted in the way rumours are, until a large section of the public had lost its faith in the Emperor. As long as Napoleon was successful in the field this defection was unimportant, but as soon as his power began to ebb it became decidedly noticeable, and, as much as anything else, helped to reconcile the mass of the people to the return of the Bourbons.

It has been well said that the man who never makes any mistakes never makes anything else, and allied to this statement is Wellington's famous dictum (which applies equally well to all kinds of endeavour) that the best general is not the one who makes fewest mistakes, but the one who takes most advantage of the mistakes of his opponent. On examining Napoleon's career one finds mistakes innumerable—and the successes are more numerous still. In military matters the explanation lies in the extreme and elaborate care Napoleon devoted to his strategic arrangements. His movements were so planned that no tactical check could derange them. His *bataillon carré* of a hundred thousand men, with Lannes the incomparable at the head of the advanced guard, could take care of itself whatever happened. The advanced guard caught the enemy and pinned him to his ground, providing that fixed point which Napoleon always desired as a pivot, and then the massed army could be wheeled with ease against whatever part of the enemy's line Napoleon selected. If victory was the result, then the pursuit was relentless; if perhaps a check was experienced, then the previous strategy had been such that the damage done was minimized. It was this system which saved him at Eylau, and which was so marvellously successful at Friedland.

The occasions when danger threatened or when disaster occurred were those when Napoleon did not act on these lines. The campaign of 1796, indeed, shows no trace of the " Napoleonic system." The principles which Napoleon followed were only those of the other generals of the period, but they were acted upon with such vigour and with such a clarity of vision that they were successful against all the odds which the Aulic Council brought to bear. At Marengo, on the other hand, the conditions were different and more exacting. This victory had to be as gratifying as possible to the French nation—it had to be gained by extraordinary means; it had to be as unlooked-for as a thunderbolt, as startling as it was successful, and it must bring prodigious results. Also (for Napoleon's own sake) it had to be gained as quickly as possible, so that he could return to Paris to overcome his enemies.

The Austrians had overrun Italy, were besieging Genoa, and had advanced to the Var. No mere frontal attack upon them would fulfil all the onerous conditions imposed upon the First Consul. A series of successes painfully gained, resulting in the slow driving of the Austrians from one river line to another, might be safe, but it would not be dramatic nor unexpected, and, worst of all, it would not be rapid. Napoleon took an enormous risk, and led his Army of Reserve over the Alps. He had satisfied the need for drama; now he had to justify himself by a speedy victory. Defeat, with an impassable defile in his rear, meant nothing less than disaster; but delay, with his enemies gradually rallying at Paris, meant similar disaster. The strain became unbearable, and Napoleon scattered his army far and wide in his endeavour to come to grips with the Austrians. The risk he ran was appalling, and was almost fatal, for the fraction of the army which he still retained under his own hand was suddenly attacked by the combined Austrians, and driven back. Napoleon flung himself into the battle; somehow he kept his battered battalions together until three undeserved strokes of luck occurred simultaneously. Desaix arrived with his stray division; Zach unduly extended the Austrian line; and Kellermann was afforded an opportunity for a decisive charge. In ten minutes the whole situation was changed. Marengo was won; it was the Austrians who were defeated without an avenue of retreat; and Napoleon was free to enjoy the intoxication of supreme power —and to meditate on the destiny which had saved him from indescribable disgrace.

The errors into which Napoleon fell during the campaign of 1805 were mainly the result of his over-estimation of his adversaries' talents. No one could possibly have imagined that Mack would have been such a spiritless fool as to stay in Ulm and allow himself to be surrounded by an army three times his strength. Napoleon certainly did not expect him to, and made his dispositions on the supposition that Mack would endeavour to fight his way through to Bohemia or Tyrol. But Mack remained paralysed; the one gap left open was closed to him by Ney's dashing victory at Elchingen, and all that remained to be done was for Napoleon to receive the timid surrender of thirty thousand men and for Murat to hunt down whatever fragments were still at large. Five weeks later the Russians were destroyed at Austerlitz. There is no manœuvre of Napoleon's during these five weeks at which anyone can reasonably cavil; the faint criticism that Napoleon ought not to have advanced as far as he did into Moravia is easily falsified by the fact that by this means he was able to find room for his retreat on Austerlitz which gave so much heart to the Russians and which induced them to make their ruinous attack on his right wing.

The mistakes which Napoleon made during the Jena campaign have already been fully discussed. He made several gross miscalculations, and his only justification is his final success. As the war went on, however, and the French advanced into Poland, we find Napoleon at his very best strategically. At Eylau he blundered in sending forward Augereau's corps in their mad rush at the powerful Russian line, but once again he was able to extricate himself from his difficulties, and Friedland settled the matter.

It is now that we come to the most disastrous adventure of all—the Spanish affair. The remark has been made that until 1808 Napoleon had only fought kings, and never a people. He plunged into the involved politics of Spain expecting as easy a victory as Masséna's conquest of Naples in 1806, or Junot's conquest of Portugal in 1807. He was sadly mistaken. And yet one can find traces indicating that he was taking all possible precautions. His instructions to his representatives at Madrid certainly suggest that he was trying to frighten the Spanish royal family out of the country, and that only when this scheme had been upset by the abdication of Charles at Aranjuez (which could not possibly have been foreseen) did he call the suicidal conference of Bayonne. The Portuguese royal family had fled from Junot; the Neapolitan Bourbons had fled from Masséna; it might have been expected that the Spanish Bourbons would have fled from Murat, especially as they had rich American dependencies in which to settle. The Spaniards would not have fought half so hard for a craven King in America as they did for one who was pictured to them as suffering a martyr's torments in a French prison. So far Napoleon's methods are perhaps justified in every way except morally. But from this time onward he made mistake after mistake. He entrusted the conquest of Spain to officers and troops of poor quality

o

—generals like Savary, Dupont and Duhesme, with mere provisional regiments formed from the sweepings of the depôts. The capitulation of Baylen and the loss of Madrid were the natural consequence. In wrath Napoleon called upon the Grand Army. He plunged into Spain, routed the wretched Spanish levies, pressed on to conquer all Spain and—was forced to wheel back to counter Moore's swift thrust at his rear.

Napoleon never returned to the Peninsula. It was not central enough; he could not from there keep an eye on the rest of Europe. He endeavoured instead to direct affairs from Paris, with the result that what little order remained dissolved into chaos. His despatches arrived six weeks late, and co-ordination was impossible. The best course left open to him was to entrust the supreme command in Spain to the most capable of his subordinates, someone who could make his plans on the spot and see that they were carried out. But there Napoleon stopped short. Give to another Frenchman the command of three hundred thousand men and all the resources of a vast kingdom? Unthinkable! So matters drifted from bad to worse while the Marshals quarrelled among themselves, while Joseph and Jourdan tried to make their authority felt, and while Napoleon blindly stirred up still further trouble among them.

Worse than this; Napoleon entirely misread the character of the Spanish war. Despite his own experiences there, he did not realize the enormous difficulties with which the French armies had to contend. He set three hundred thousand men a task which would have kept half a million fully occupied, and he further hampered them by the niggardly nature of their allowances of money and material. He under-estimated the fighting power of the guerillas, of the Portuguese levies, and (worst of all) of the English army. He over-estimated the

MASSENA
(PRINCE D'ESSLING AND DUC DE RIVOLI)

power of his name among the unlettered Spanish peasants. He left entirely out of account the impossibility of communication and of supply. In a word, there was no error open to him into which he did not fall.

The Spanish trouble had hardly assumed serious dimensions when in 1809 Austria made one more bid for freedom and commenced hostilities against him. As busy as he could possibly be with Spanish affairs, with troubles in Paris, and with ruling the rest of Europe, Napoleon delayed before going in person to the seat of war. He miscalculated the time necessary to Austria to mobilize, and he entrusted the temporary command to Berthier—two grave errors. Only Davout's skill and his own unconquerable energy staved off a serious disaster and snatched a victory from the jaws of defeat. The French pressed on to Vienna. This time there was no Auersperg to be cozened out of his command of the Danube bridge; the crossings were all broken down, and Napoleon was compelled to force a passage in face of a hostile army of equal strength—the most delicate operation known to military science. Napoleon's first attempt was rash to the verge of madness. It was simply a blind thrust at the heart of the opposing army; the bridges provided were insufficient, and broke down through enemy action at the crisis of the battle; the staff work and the arrangements generally appear to have been defective. Thirty-six hours of fierce fighting saw the French hurled back again; Masséna's tenacity and Lannes' daring saved the army from destruction, but the cost of defeat amounted to twenty thousand men—among them was Lannes, the hero of Montebello, of Saalfeld, of Friedland, of Saragossa; one of the few who dared to say what they thought to the Emperor, and one of the few who enjoyed his trust and friendship.

To point the moral, Napoleon contrived soon afterwards to bring up huge reinforcements, and then to cross the Danube without opposition. The movement was carefully planned and carried out, and the results were the victory of Wagram, the armistice of Znaim, and the dismemberment of Austria. If, after experiencing a severe defeat, Napoleon could succeed in bringing up the Army of Italy and crossing the Danube without opposition, he could surely have done so at the first attempt. The battle of Aspern is typical of Napoleon's reckless methods and of his under-estimation of the enemy.

In this campaign of 1809 Napoleon's fall was nearly anticipated. Had the forty thousand men whom England sent to Walcheren, too late, been despatched a little earlier, under a competent general; had Prussia flung her weight into the scale at the same time, it is hard to see how Napoleon could have recovered himself. Germany was already prepared to revolt, Tyrol was ablaze with insurrection, Wellington was marching into the heart of Spain, Russia was ready to change sides at a moment's notice. What saved Napoleon was the fact that three of his enemies were timid and incompetent. Chatham could achieve nothing in the Netherlands; Frederick William III. hesitated in Prussia, and Francis of Austria, although Wagram was not in the least a crushing defeat, decided that he could not continue the struggle.

We have already dealt in part with 1812 and 1813. There are mistakes in plenty here, although now they were accentuated by the worst of ill luck. The whole advance into Russia was one gigantic error; not even Napoleon's tremendous efforts could counter-balance the handicaps which he encountered, and which he ought to have foreseen. As far back as 1807 he had commented bitterly on the horrible Polish roads and on the clinging black mud of that district; he should have realized that it was impossible for him to feed an army five hundred thousand strong by road transport under such conditions. Neverthe-less, he nearly succeeded at Smolensk in countering a strategic disadvantage by a tactical victory, in the same manner as he had done twelve years before at Marengo. Even after utter ruin had descended upon him, he contrived by his gigantic labours to raise a new army and to enter afresh into the field in 1813 before his enemies were ready for him. The early movements in the campaign are practically perfect; until after Bautzen he showed all his old brilliancy and skill—negatived this time by the mistakes of subordinates. But from Bautzen onwards we find repeated errors both in policy and in the field. It was a mistake to enter into the armistice of Pleisswitz; it was a mistake not to secure the neutrality of Austria, even if it had cost him the whole Kingdom of Italy; it was a mistake not to accept the Allies' offers of peace; it was a mistake not to send back Ferdinand to Spain and extricate himself somehow from the tangle of the Peninsular War; it was a mistake to send Oudinot and Ney against Berlin; it was a mistake to try to hold the line of the Elbe; it was a mistake to fight at Leipzig; and, having decided to fight, it was a mistake not to see that there was a satisfactory line of retreat over the Elster.

It is clear that Napoleon was not the man he once was. And yet—and yet he nearly saved the whole situation at Dresden! Three days' fighting there nearly counter-balanced all the disasters of the previous eighteen months. Smolensk, Bautzen and Dresden—three times he almost made up for all his defeats. The conclusion is forced upon one that all through the years of victory Napoleon was on the verge of defeat, and all through the years of defeat he was on the verge of victory. For twenty years the fate of Europe hung balanced upon a razor edge.

Napoleon's good luck is very evident; his bad luck was an equally potent factor in his career. On striking a balance and considering what enormous success was his for a time, the resultant inference is unavoidable. He was vastly superior to all the other men of his time; his superiority was such that individual differences between others fade into insignificance when contrasted with the difference between him and anyone else who may be selected for comparison. He was superior not merely in mental capacity, but in all other qualities necessary for success in any sphere of business. His moral courage was enormous; his finesse and rapidity of thought were unequalled. He hardly knew what it was to despair. His adaptability and his fertility of resource were amazing.

In spite of this (or perhaps because of this) it is very easy to detract from any of his achievements. The Code Napoléon, his most enduring monument, was not his own work, nor, of course, can much credit be given to his assistants. Codification of laws is in no way a new idea—it is almost contemporary with laws themselves. Napoleon's German policy was much the same as that of Louis XIV.; his Italian policy is reminiscent of Charles VIII.'s or even earlier; the germ of his Oriental policy can be found in that of Louis IX.; his Spanish policy was similar to, but more unsuccessful than that of his predecessors. Even the Continental system was only the development of previous schemes to their logical climax. In his Court arrangements Napoleon brought no new idea into play; most of his regulations were elaborated from the ceremony which surrounded the Soleil Monarque, while others were borrowed from the etiquette of the courts of Vienna and Madrid. Any

approaching ceremony called for an anxious examination of precedents; if Napoleon could find a parallel
far back stamped with the approval of a Valois or
an Orléans-Angoulême the matter was settled on
the same lines, no matter what inconveniences
resulted. Similarly in purely Imperial concerns he
was always harking back to Charlemagne or to the
Empire of Rome. It is exceedingly probable that
his annexation of Spain north of the Ebro in 1812,
which excited roars of derision all over Europe
because three-quarters of the district was aflame with
guerillas who shot on sight any Frenchman they
met, was directly inspired by Charlemagne's action
a thousand years before. Charlemagne's Spanish
campaign, even if it added the Spanish March to
his dominions, cost him his rearguard and all his
Paladins; Napoleon might well have taken warning.
The references to Imperial Rome, from the design
of his coinage and the plan of the Arc de Triomphe
to the " cohorts " of the National Guard and his
adoption of Eugène, are too numerous to mention.
We even find him going back farther still, and complaining that he could not, like Alexander, announce
himself as of divine birth and the son of Jupiter.

In military matters an equally well (or ill) founded
charge of unoriginality can be brought against
Napoleon's methods. To those of us who saw a
short time ago what changes four years of war
wrought in the weapons and tactics employed, it
seems amazing that at the end of twenty years of
life and death struggles the soldiers were still armed
with the smooth bore flintlock musket which had
already been in use for a century. Only two
important new weapons were evolved, and neither
of them attained any great popularity. They were
shrapnel shell and military rockets, and the latter, at
least, Napoleon never employed. The rifle never
attained any popularity with him, although to us it

seems obvious that it was the weapon of the future.
Fulton offered Napoleon his steamboat invention,
and was treated as a wild dreamer—at the very time
when Napoleon was most preoccupied with the
problem of sending an army across the Channel.
As an irresponsible autocrat, Napoleon had bound-
less opportunities of testing and employing any
new invention which might be suggested, but he
made no use of them.   In this respect he compares
unfavourably with his far less gifted nephew.
Napoleon III.'s system of "sausages and cham-
pagne" certainly finds a parallel in his uncle's treatment of his troops when not on active service.
When Napoleon's armies returned victorious they
were received with fêtes and salutes innumerable; an
ignorant observer might well have believed them to
be demigods, to whom ceremonies and sacrifices
were peculiarly acceptable.   The arrangement had
a double effect; it is certainly good for an army's
esprit de corps for the men to be considered demigods; and it is certainly useful for an autocrat whose
rule is based on his army to have his subjects believe
that that army is semi-divine.   But for the little
personal comforts of his men Napoleon took small
notice.   They were not relieved of the cumbersome
features of their uniforms; even if they were not
worried by petty details of pipeclay and brass polish
as were the English, they were still forced to wear
the horrible stock and tunic which Frederick the
Great had set in fashion.   The French army slang
term "bleu" for recruit has its origin in the fact
that the recruits for the old army used to go black
and blue in the face owing to the unaccustomed
restriction of the Napoleonic stock.   The French
helmets may have been imposing, but they were
terribly uncomfortable to wear.   The gain in
efficiency resulting from a radical change in these
matters must have counter-balanced any possible loss

in esprit de corps had Napoleon seen fit to bring this change about.

It is with trembling and delicacy that one approaches the realm in which Napoleon apparently reigns supreme—that of tactics. It is a rash act to say that the winner of sixty battles won them badly. Yet one cannot help making a few cautious comments. When Napoleon attained supreme power the line and the column were almost equally in favour in the French army. The most usual formation in action was the line, backed at intervals by the column. At Marengo this arrangement was largely employed, and was successful. As time went on, however, we find that the line disappeared, its place was taken by additional skirmishers, and the columns became heavier and heavier. The system was altogether vicious; the column is both untrustworthy and expensive. French columns might be successful when pitted against any other columns, but they failed against disciplined infantry formed in line. Every battle and combat fought by the English, from Alexandria and Maida to Vittoria, proved this, but Napoleon and his officers never learnt the lesson. The Emperor's letters to his generals in Spain give repeated examples of his contempt for the English and Portuguese troops; it was hardly a contempt that was justified. And despite all these warnings, despite (so it is reported) Soult's and Foy's pleadings, the first grand attack at Waterloo was made by twenty thousand infantry herded together twenty-four deep. This clumsy mass was easily held up, outflanked and forced back by six thousand English and Hanoverians under Picton. It was not the first example which had been forced upon Napoleon's notice of the uselessness of the column. At Wagram he had sent Macdonald's corps, some twenty thousand strong, against the Austrian centre, massed in a gigantic hollow square, which can be considered as forming two columns each about thirty-five deep. Macdonald reached his objective, but by the time he arrived his men were so jostled together, ploughed up by artillery, and generally demoralized that they could effect nothing. One lesson such as this ought to have convinced Napoleon, but it did not. He continued to use columns—and he was beaten at Waterloo. It is frequently urged in his defence that the column was the "natural" formation in the French army, that tradition had grown up around it, so that it was unsafe to meddle with it, that French troops fight better in column than in line, and that his troops were of necessity so raw that they could not be trusted in line. These arguments seem completely nullified by the facts that the line was actually employed early in Napoleon's career, that both before and after Waterloo French troops fought well in line, and that at Waterloo, at any rate, the French troops were all well-trained, while Picton's men were largely new recruits.

The employment of cavalry in the Imperial armies might similarly be condemned as extravagant and inefficient. The system of Seidlitz under Frederick the Great was forgotten. Napoleon had uprooted the triumphal memorial erected at Rossbach, and with it it seemed he had uprooted the memory of the charges with which Seidlitz' hardwelded squadrons had routed the army of France fifty years before. Murat's famous charges were not pressed home in the hard, utterly logical fashion of Frederick's cavalry. If the opposing infantry stood firm at the approach of the cavalry, then the latter parted and drifted away down each flank. If (as must be admitted was much more usual) the infantry broke at the sight of the horsemen tearing down on them, then the pursuit was pushed home remorselessly, but never do we find the perfect charge, in few ranks, packed close together and held together like a steel chain, which must overturn everything in its way. Under Napoleon the French cavalry never charged home; at Waterloo we find the great cavalry charges, which Ney directed against the English squares, made at a trot, and the horsemen, swerving from the steel-rimmed, fire-spouting squares, wandering idly about on the flanks, while a few of the more enterprising cut feebly at the bayonets with their sabres. Wellington's description of them riding about as if they owned the place argues powerfully against their ever having flung themselves upon the bayonet points, as good cavalry should do if sent against unbroken infantry.

In fact, both the French infantry and the French cavalry relied upon the moral effect of their advance rather than upon their capacity for doing damage when they made their charges. It is perfectly true that they were generally successful; Napoleon's dictum that the moral is to the physical as three to one was borne out in a hundred battles from Arcola to Dresden; but it was found wanting at Vimiero, at Busaco, at Borodino, at Waterloo, everywhere in fact, where the enemy was too stubborn or well-disciplined to flinch from the waving sabres or the grenadiers' gigantic head-dresses.

In the wider field of strategy it cannot be denied that Napoleon made use of original devices and brought about revolutionary changes in the whole system. They do not appear in the Italian campaign of 1796 nor in the campaigns of Egypt and Marengo, but in 1805 we find the cavalry screen completely contrived and in efficient working order; in 1806 the strategic advanced guard; and in 1807 the perfect combination of the two. The curious part is that Napoleon himself did not seem to realize the importance of his own inventions; time and again in 1812 and 1813 he did not employ them, with invariably disastrous results. It seems a mistake on Napoleon's part not to have made use of the new devices on these occasions, but it is unwise to condemn him offhand, because it seems inconceivable that he of all persons did not appreciate the magnitude and efficiency of his own discoveries; there must have been some reason not now apparent for these actions.

It is very nearly impossible to discover any action of Napoleon's which was not faulty in some way, or which could not be improved upon. But since he met with unprecedented success the only conclusion is that, although his mistakes were many, they were far fewer than would have been the average man's. Furthermore, since his schemes were all so direct and simple (a comparison between his plan and Moreau's for the crossing of the Rhine at Schaffhausen in 1800 is very illuminating on this point), no one can help feeling a sneaking suspicion, when reading of Napoleon's achievements, that he could not have done the same—only just a little better. Thiers' long-drawn panegyric grows ineffably wearisome simply on this account; the writer's efforts to minimize his hero's errors are so obvious and so ineffective that the reader is irritated by them, while the continued superlatives seem to be given with gross unfairness to a man whose blunders are so difficult to conceal. It is far easier to write a panegyric on a man who has done nothing whatever than on a man whose whole life was spent in productive activity.

Of what has sometimes been termed Napoleon's cardinal error, the Continental System, I have not ventured to speak. As originally conceived it was undoubtedly a wise move. If France could exist without English products, then obviously it was a sound proceeding to deprive England of so rich a market for her goods. The complications make the question much more difficult. Certainly the effort to close the whole of Europe to British trade led Napoleon into damaging annexations and disastrous wars, while the fact that the countries involved, Russia, for instance, preferred to fight rather than to continue to enforce the system, seems to indicate that it was impossible to enforce—that the country (or at least its Government) could not continue to exist without British trade. This is the simplest complication of all. It is when we come to consider Napoleon's juggling with permits and licenses that we become involved in the fog which surrounds all tariff questions. The only certain points are that Napoleon derived a large revenue from his licenses, that the British Government was frequently severely embarrassed for want of money (the difficulties involved in collecting sufficient gold to pay subsidies and the expenses of armies in the field led to unfortunate delays), and that the discontent of the Continent was great and general. It is a purely arbitrary matter, dependent on the personal equation, to come to any decision as to the balance of these conclusions.

Taking the career of Napoleon as a whole, it is easy to see how frequently he was guilty of errors; what should also be obvious is that it was almost inevitable that he should fall into these errors. If the Austrian marriage was a mistake, then it was a mistake Napoleon could not help making; undoubtedly he did the best he could for himself in the prevailing circumstances. If the advance into Russia was a mistake, it is impossible to indicate what alternative could have been chosen, for Napoleon, at war with Russia, could not safely remain at war without gaining a decision; he could hardly maintain an army on the Russian frontier awaiting Alexander's pleasure.

If it was a mistake to advance into Belgium in

June, 1815, it would have been a far worse one not to have advanced. The greatest mistake of those into which he was *not* driven by circumstances was his theft of the throne of Spain—and it was that which ruined him.

CHAPTER XVII

ST. HELENA

WHEN Napoleon abdicated after Waterloo, for the second time, the Allies had achieved the object for which ostensibly they had made war. The Emperor had fallen, and the war they had waged had, they declared, been directed entirely against him. The immediate and burning question now arose as to what was to be done with the man against whom a million other men were on the march. Blücher wanted to catch him and shoot him; Wellington, with his usual cautious good sense, did not want to be burdened with the responsibility of an action which might be unnecessary and would certainly be unpopular. Napoleon himself, disowned by the government and by the army, wanted to retire to America, but his enemies were unwilling to set him free. The English fleet blockaded the coast, and Napoleon was compelled to surrender to it, lest worse should befall from the Prussians, or the Republicans, or the White Terror, or from personal enemies. He tried to make the best of his necessity by claiming the hospitality of England, but England kept him a close prisoner until her Allies had been consulted. They offered to hand him over to Louis XVIII. for trial as a rebel, but even Louis had the sense to decline the offer. He could shoot Ney and la Bédoyère, but he could not shoot Napoleon. For

223

Louis to shut him up in a fortress would be as
dangerous as it would be for a private individual to
keep a tiger in his cellar.   In the same way no
Continental state would willingly see any other
appointed his guardian. That would mean giving
the guardian country a most potent instrument of
menace.   England remained the sole possible gaoler,
and England accepted the responsibility.

Next arose the question as to the locality of
the prison, and the answer to that question was
already prepared—St. Helena. To keep Napoleon
in England was obviously impossible, for England
was nearer France even than was Elba, while,
incredible though it might seem, the oligarchy
which ruled England were afraid lest Napoleon
should corrupt the mass of the people to Republicanism. That there was some foundation for this
fear is shown by the intense interest in Napoleon
which the people displayed while he was in Plymouth
harbour. Similar arguments were effective against
Malta or any other Mediterranean island.   But
St. Helena had none of these disadvantages.   It
was thousands of miles away; it was small, and could
be filled with troops; there were only two possible
places for landing, and these could be well guarded;
the few reports on the island which were to be had
seemed to indicate that fair comfort was obtainable
there, and, above all, it was not at all a place where
ships or individuals could easily find an excuse for
calling or remaining. Even before the descent from
Elba St. Helena had been suggested as a more
suitable place for Napoleon's prison, and now, with
little discussion, he was sent off there.

It is impossible to argue about the legality or
otherwise of this decision. Morally, the Powers
were as justified in imprisoning Napoleon as is a
government in locking up a homicidal maniac. A
maniac may hurt people; Napoleon might hurt the

Powers. Napoleon might hurt them for reasons which to him might appear perfectly defensible; but a homicidal maniac can usually boast the same purity of motive. The maniac may be right and everyone else wrong; Napoleon may have been right and the Powers wrong; but the Powers were none the less justified in seeing that he could do no more harm. It has been argued that by invading France and removing her ruler Europe was committing a moral crime; that it is intolerable for one country to interfere in another country's system of government. This argument fails because its scope is inelastic. In the same way it is said that "an Englishman's house is his castle," and that, for instance, a man's conduct towards, or training of, his children is his own personal business. But if that man tries to cut his children's throats, or worse, encourages his children to cut his neighbours' throats, then the State steps in and prevents him from doing so. That is exactly what the Powers did with Napoleon. Where they went wrong was in not seeing that their decision was carried into effect with humanity and dignity.

The initial arrangements for Napoleon's exile seemed to portend that he would end his days in luxury. Lord Liverpool had said that on the island there was a most comfortable house exactly suited for Napoleon and his suite; Lord Bathurst had given official orders that he was to be allowed all possible indulgence so long as his detention was not imperilled. But Napoleon was not given the comfortable house, while Bathurst's confidential orders to Sir Hudson Lowe displayed unbelievable rigour. Already Napoleon had experienced some of the results of the workings of the official mind; the naval officers with whom he had come in contact had been strictly ordered not to pay him any of the compliments usually accorded to royalty. They remained covered in his presence, and they addressed

P

him as "General Bonaparte." Cockburn, the
Admiral in command, acted strictly to the letter
of the orders which commanded him to treat
" General Bonaparte " in the same manner as he
would a general officer not in employ. If Napoleon
seemed inclined to act with more dignity than this
rather humble station would warrant, then Cockburn
was distant and reserved ; but if Napoleon ever showed
signs of " conducting himself with modesty," as
Cockburn himself writes, then the Admiral was
graciously pleased to unbend a little to his helpless
prisoner.

The whole question of the title was intricate and
irritating. The English Government declared that
they had never recognized Napoleon as Emperor even
at the height of his power, and they certainly were
not going to do so now that he was a discredited
outcast. They were hardly correct in fact or in
theory, for they had sent him an Ambassador when
he was First Consul ; they had sent plenipotentiaries
to Châtillon who had signed documents in which he
was called Emperor ; they h￢ 1 sent a representative
to him at Elba when he was Emperor there, and,
equally important, they had ratified the Convention
of Cintra, among the documents of which he was
distinctly called His Imperial Majesty. Moreover,
by refusing him this mode of address, they were
insulting the French people, who had elected him,
the Courts of Europe, who had recognized him, and
the Pope, who had crowned and anointed him. It
was the English Government which lost its dignity
in this ridiculous affair, not Napoleon. But the
worst result of this decision was not the loss of
dignity, nor the injury to French pride. It was that
it gave Napoleon an opportunity to hit back. It
gave him a definite cause of complaint, apart from
that of his arbitrary incarceration, which was
generally held to be justified. It was the first

opportunity of many, of all of which Napoleon eagerly took advantage, so that the Napoleonic Legend had a firm base for future development. By complaining at any and every opportunity Napoleon was able to surround his own memory with an aura of frightful privations, so that it was easy for his subtle nephew later to picture him as Prometheus, the benefactor of mankind, bound to his rock in mid-ocean with the vultures of the allied commissioners gnawing at his liver.

A further blunder on the part of the English Government afforded Napoleon his next cause of complaint. Sir Hudson Lowe was a good, if unimaginative soldier who had fought all his life against the French. Furthermore, he had commanded a force of Corsican Rangers, recruited from the island that was Napoleon's birthplace. He had held Capri for two years in the face of Masséna and Joseph Bonaparte, and was only turned out by a daring expedition sent by Murat. His very name was hateful to Napoleon, and yet he was appointed his guardian. But this was not all. A huge responsibility devolved upon Sir Hudson Lowe. A moment's carelessness on his part might allow Napoleon to escape, and if Napoleon escaped there might ensue another Waterloo campaign with a very different result. The responsibility was too great altogether for Lowe. Because of it he carried out the orders sent him with a strictness which knew no bounds. He pestered the wretched prisoner, who already had good reason to dislike him, until he nearly drove him frantic. Lowe himself was desperate, and many people who saw him during that period commented on his worried demeanour and his inability to support his responsibilities. It is easy then to imagine the violent friction which prevailed between him and his captive.

On a casual inspection, the restrictions imposed

upon Napoleon do not seem particularly severe. He
was to keep within certain limits; he was to be
accompanied by an English officer if he went beyond
them; his correspondence was to pass through
Lowe's hands, and he was to assure the English of
his presence every day.   But these restrictions galled
Napoleon inexpressibly.   Along the boundaries of
his free area was posted a line of sentries, and he
could not turn his eyes in any direction without
perceiving the hated redcoats.   The continued
presence of an officer if he rode elsewhere was
not unnaturally irksome—so irksome, in fact, that
Napoleon, who had previously passed half his days
on horseback, gave up riding—while the mortification
of having his letters pried into and the utter, hateful
humiliation of having to exhibit himself on command
to an Englishman must have been maddening to a
man who not so many months before had ruled half
Europe.

Napoleon found himself shut up in a restricted
area and with limited accommodation; he had no old
friends with him, because he had never had any
friends; of the five officers who had accompanied
him only two were men of any distinction and of
any length of service.   Not one of them was
particularly talented, and they were one and all
fiercely jealous of each other.   Add to these
conditions a tropical climate and the utter despair
into which they were all plunged, and it is easy to
realize that furious quarrels and bitter heart-burn-
ings must have been their lot.   It is the most
difficult matter in the world to find the exact truth
about what went on in Longwood.   Everyone concerned wrote voluminously, and everyone concerned
wrote accounts which differed from everyone else's.
There is an atmosphere of untruth surrounding
everything which has been written by the actors in
this last tragedy.   Napoleon himself set his friends

the example, for his dictated memoirs and the information which he gave Las Cases to help him in his writings are full of lies, some cunning, some clumsy, but all of them devised for obvious purposes. He tried to throw the blame of the Spanish insurrection on Murat, the blame of the execution of d'Enghien on Talleyrand, the blame of Waterloo on Grouchy. It is difficult to discover whether he was merely trying to excuse himself in the eyes of the world, or to rehabilitate Bonapartism so that his son might eventually mount the Imperial throne. And his companions' memoirs lie so blatantly and so obviously that one cannot decide which was his aim.

Napoleon himself had deteriorated vastly. As might be expected, his complete cessation of bodily activity led to an increase in his corpulence until he became gross and unwieldy. His mental power had decayed, although he was still able to dictate for hours on end. Even under the burdensome conditions imposed upon him he never seems to have abandoned the rigid reserve which he had maintained all his life. The few scenes which the memoirists describe which have a ring of truth about them seem to show him still acting a part, still posing as the inestimably superior being whom his followers believed him to be. Sometimes we have a brief glimpse of him stripped of his heroics, as witness the occasion when he said bitterly that his son must necessarily have forgotten him; but most of the time he seems to have adhered to his old methods, and posed as the misunderstood benefactor of humanity, ignoring Marie Louise's defection, ignoring the distrust with which the Council of State had regarded him during the last months of his reign; in fact proclaiming himself the man who martyred himself for the French nation, with such iteration that he was at last believed. His declamations have coloured nearly everything written since, so that it is quite usual to find it stated, either actually or inferentially, that his fall was due solely to the jealousy of the other rulers of Europe, and not due in any degree to the slowly developed dislike of his own subjects.

And all this time he was making Sir Hudson Lowe's life a burden to him as well. Some of Napoleon's complaints were just, some merely frivolous, but every one of them goaded Lowe into further painful activity. This activity reacted in another direction, so that Lowe issued edicts of increased stringency, and, half mad with responsibility, treated Napoleon with an exaggeration of precaution and imposed upon him restraints of a pettiness and a casuistry almost unbelievable. It can hardly be doubted that Napoleon actually sought opportunities for egging Lowe on to further ill-treatment; he certainly treated him with a most amazing contumely, and it is very probable that the numerous rumours of attempts at rescue, by submarine boat, by an armed force from Brazil, or by any other fantastic means, had their origin in Napoleon himself, so that Lowe was inspired to further obnoxious measures. Napoleon made the most of his opportunity. He raised a clamour which reached Europe (as he had intended), so that interest in his fate and sympathy for the poor ill-treated captive gradually worked up to fever heat. He sold his plate to buy himself necessaries (at a time when he had ample money at his command) and of course France heard about it, and was wrung with pity for the wretched man forced by his captor's rapacity to dine off earthenware. The fact that Napoleon nevertheless retained sufficient silver to supply his table was not so readily divulged. He made a continual complaint about his health; undoubtedly he was not well, and equally undoubtedly he was already suffer-

LOUIS NAPOLEON, KING OF HOLLAND

ing from the disease which killed him; but his complaints were neither consistent nor, as far as can be ascertained, entirely true. He hinted that the Powers were endeavouring to shorten his life; he even said that he went in fear of assassins. All this news reached Europe by devious routes, and sympathy grew and grew until, after the lapse of years, it waxed into the hysteria evinced at his second funeral and the more effective hysteria which set Napoleon III. on the throne.

Despite all the undignified squabbles in which he was engaged, one can nevertheless hardly restrain a feeling of admiration for Napoleon amid the trials which he was enduring. He was hitting back as hard as circumstances would allow him, and he was hitting back with effect. He had driven Lowe frantic, and he had secured his object of reviving European interest in him. Furthermore, he flatly refused to submit to the humiliating commands which Lowe attempted to enforce. Lowe might speak of "General Bonaparte" or "Napoleon Bonaparte" (in the same way as he might speak of John Robinson, says Lord Rosebery) but in his own home Napoleon was always His Imperial Majesty the Emperor, to whom everyone uncovered, and in whose presence everyone remained standing. Lowe's order that he must show himself to an English officer every day was completely ignored, and we hear of officers climbing trees and peering through keyholes in vain attempts to make sure of his presence. For days together Napoleon might have been out of the island for all Lowe knew to the contrary. The commissioners sent by France and Austria and Russia did not set eyes on him from the time of their arrival until after his death. Napoleon had sworn that he would shoot with his own hand the first man who intruded on his privacy, and he was believed; the attempt was never made, and Napoleon continued to reign in Longwood, in an *imperium in imperio.*

The whole period seems indescribably sordid and wretched. Napoleon's companions were intriguing jealously for his favour, scheming for the privilege of eating at his table, and even endeavouring to be sure that he would leave them his money in his will. Tropical weather, harassing conditions, prolonged strain, and the overwhelming gloom of recent frightful disasters, all tended towards overstrained nerves and continual quarrels. Napoleon wrangling with Lowe over his dinner-service; Montholon in tears because Napoleon chooses to dine with Las Cases; an Emperor quarrelling with a general as to whether or not his liver is enlarged; this is not tragedy, it is only squalor with a hideously tragic taint. It is Lear viewed through reversed opera-glasses.

The end came at last in 1821. The disease of which his father had died held Napoleon as well in its grip. He was an intractable patient, and diagnosis was not easy, but it certainly seems that the medical treatment he received was unspeakably bad. He was dosed with tartar emetic, of all drugs, at a time when his stomach was deranged with cancer. At times he suffered frightful agony. He bore it somehow; argued with his doctors, chaffed his friends, until at last he sank into unconsciousness, and he died while a great storm howled round the island. The lies and contradictions of the memoirists persist even here, for no one knows accurately what were his last words, or when they were uttered.

The post-mortem report is sufficient to convince any reader that none of the doctors concerned knew their business;[1] the man who had once ruled Europe

[1] It is, I believe, a fact never previously published that the first post-mortem certificate drawn up by the doctors responsible was rejected by Sir Hudson Lowe. It contained the words " the liver was perhaps a little

was now thrust into a coffin too small to allow him to wear his complete uniform, so that his hat rested on his stomach; and he was buried in one of his old favourite spots in the island. Once more there arose the old vexed question of title, for the French wished to inscribe "Napoleon" on the coffin; Lowe insisted on "Bonaparte" being added; in the end it was a nameless coffin which was lowered into the grave.

Napoleon failed during his lifetime, but he was triumphant after death. His gallant fight at St. Helena against overwhelming odds was remembered with pride by every Frenchman. Men hearing garbled versions of his sufferings felt a pricking of their consciences that they had abandoned him in 1814 and 1815. The helpless policy of Louis XVIII. and Charles X., and the humdrum policy of Louis Philippe set all minds thinking of the glorious days, not so very long ago, when France had been Queen of the Continent. Louis Napoleon skilfully employed the revulsion of feeling to his own advantage, and the glory of Austerlitz and Jena was sufficient to hide the absurdities of Boulogne and Strasbourg. But it was the six years' struggle of St. Helena which made so refulgent that glory of Austerlitz.

What the British Government could have done to prevent the formation of a St. Helena legend cannot easily be decided. They were in terror lest he should escape again, and severe ordinances were

larger than natural," and this remark naturally did not commend itself to Lowe, in consequence of the fierce quarrels he had had with Napoleon on this very subject. The post-mortem certificate in the English Record Office does not contain these words, but the Rev. Canon E. Brook Jackson, Rector of Streatham, has in his possession the earlier certificate, signed by the doctors concerned, with the footnote " N.B.—The words obliterated were suppressed by order of Sir Hudson Lowe. Signed, Thomas Short, P.M.O." The words referred to are clearly legible and are those given above.

necessary to prevent this. Had they treated him luxuriously, public opinion in England would have been roused to a dangerous pitch. They had originally tried to get out of the difficulty by handing him over to Louis XVIII. for execution, but Louis XVIII. had no real case against him. A state trial would have given Napoleon unbounded opportunities for the rhetoric in which he delighted, and which had so often rallied France to his side. Napoleon might well have pleaded, with perfect truth, that in the descent from Elba he was no rebel, but the Emperor of Elba making war upon the King of France; but so tame a plea would hardly have been employed. Napoleon would have proclaimed himself the purest altruist come to see that the French people obtained their rights, or to save France from the machinations of tyrants. Louis was wise in refusing the offer. The custody of Napoleon was thus thrust upon the British Government. If remarkably far-sighted, they might have lapped him in every luxury; have treated him subserviently as if he was Emperor in fact as well as in name; they might have encouraged him to debauchery as wild as Tiberius' at Capri; and then by subtle propaganda they might have exhibited him to a scornful world as a man who cared nothing for his lost greatness, or for the dependence of his position. Such a scheme appealed favourably to the imagination, but there was an insuperable obstacle—Napoleon. Napoleon had a definite plan of campaign. He was going to complain about everything and everybody with whom he came in contact. He was going to clamour unceasingly against the brutality and arbitrariness of his gaolers. Without regard for truth he was going to proclaim continually that he was being ill-treated and martyred, and he would have done it whatever had been his treatment, and, being Napoleon, he would have done it well. The error of the British Government lay in their affording him so many opportunities, not in their affording him any at all.

And after he was dead there followed the events which he had foreseen and over whose engendering he had laboured so diligently. Little by little the evil features of the Imperial régime were forgotten; the glory of his victories blazed more brightly in comparison with the exhaustion of France under the Bourbons and the pettifogging Algerian razzias of Louis Philippe. The literature of St. Helena, both the spurious and the inspired, induced men to believe that Napoleon was the exact opposite of what he really was. It gave him credit for the achievements of Carnot; it shifted the disgrace of failure on to the shoulders of helpless scapegoats. It proved to the satisfaction of the uninquiring that Napoleon stood for democracy, for the principle of nationality, and even for peace. It raised to the Imperial throne the man who said "the Empire means peace." The whole legend which developed was a flagrant denial of patent facts, but it was a denial sufficiently reiterated to be believed. The belief is not yet dead.

APPENDIX

INCIDENTS AND AUTHORITIES

IT is much more than a hundred years since Napoleon lived; since his time we have witnessed cataclysms more vast than were the Napoleonic wars; the Europe of that period seems to us as unfamiliar and as profitless a study as Siam or primitive Australia. Perhaps this is so. Perhaps the lessons to be drawn from the Napoleonic era are now exhausted. Perhaps the epoch ushered in by Marengo is slight and unimportant compared to that which follows the Marne. Perhaps Englishmen will forget the men who stood firm in the squares at Waterloo, and will only remember those who stood firm at Ypres and the Second Marne. Perhaps the Congress of Vienna will lapse into insignificance when compared with the Congress of Versailles. But this is inconceivable. Previously, perhaps, too much importance has been attached to the Napoleonic era, but that is because it had no parallel; it was unique. Similarly the period pivoting about the Great War of 1914-18 might be said to be unique, but it is not so. The two epochs are very closely related, very closely indeed. Much may be gained from the study of either, but this is nothing to be compared with the gain resulting from the study and comparison of the two together. In this way the Napoleonic era becomes more significant even than it was before the great war, and this without considering how much of the great war was directly due to arrangements made as a consequence of Napoleon's career.

But apart from all such considerations, the study of the period is one from which a great deal of purely personal pleasure can be derived. Even nowadays one cannot help a thrill of excitement when reading of the advance of the British infantry at Albuera; one cannot help feeling a surge of emotion on reading how Alvarez at the siege of Gerona moaned " No surrender! No surrender! " although he was dying of fever and half the populace lay dead in the streets, while the other half still fought on against all the might of Reille and St. Cyr. Even the best novel compares unfavourably with Ségur's account of the Russian campaign; and although there is no French biographer quite as good as Boswell, yet there are scores of memoirs and biographies of the period which rank very nearly as high, and which are pleasant to read at all times. Marbot may be untruthful, but he is delightful reading; Madame Junot gives a picture of her times and of the people whom she met which is honestly worthy of comparison with Dickens and Thackeray; while to track down in their memoirs Fouché's and Talleyrand's carefully concealed mistakes is as interesting a pastime as ever was the attempt to guess the dénouement in a modern detective novel.

The literature of the time is full of happy anecdotes, some of which have attained the supreme honour of being taken out bodily, furnished with modern trimmings, and published in twentieth century magazines, without acknowledgment, as modern humour. But many have escaped this fate, partly because they are untranslatable, and partly because they bear the definite imprint of the period. Thus there is the story of the fat and pursy King of Würtemberg, who once kept waiting a committee of the Congress of Vienna. At last he arrived, and as his portly majesty came bustling through the door, Talleyrand remarked, " Here comes the King of Würtemberg, *ventre à terre.*" In a grimmer vein is the story of the reception held on the night after Ney was shot. The company

were mournfully discussing the tragedy, when a certain
M. Lemaréchal was announced. As this gentleman had
a son of mature years, the announcement was worded
" M.   Lemaréchal   ainé " — which   the   panic-stricken
assembly heard as " M. le Maréchal Ney."

Some of the heroes of that time have had the bad
luck to be misrepresented not only in literature but even
in portraits and in sculpture. Napoleon had at one time
the plan of placing statues of all his generals in the
Louvre, but he abdicated before the work was anywhere
near completion, and left its continuation to his successors.
Louis and Charles did nothing towards it, and the
parsimonious Louis Philippe, when he came to the throne,
decided as a measure of economy only to represent the
most famous. But some of the statues of junior officers
were already finished. Louis Philippe saw his chance of
still greater economy. For Lasalle's head was substituted
Lannes'; for Colbert's, Mortier's; while the entire statue
of St. Hilaire was simply labelled Masséna and set up
without further alteration. These statues are still in the
Louvre; no subsequent correction has ever been made.

But the anecdotes are responsible for only a very
small part of the interest of Napoleonic literature. Many
of the subsequent histories are very nearly models of
everything a book ought to be. Napier's " Peninsular
War," despite its bias and its frequent inaccuracies, has
already become a classic; Sir Charles Oman's work on the
same subject is much more striking and makes a far
greater appeal. His descriptions of the siege of Gerona
and of the cavalry pursuit at Tudela are more moving in
their cold eloquence than ever was Napier at his fieriest.
One English author whose books have attracted far less
attention than they should have done is Mr. F. Loraine
Petre; his accurate and impartial histories of the
successive Napoleonic campaigns are dramatic enough to
hold the interest of the ordinary reader as well as that of
the military student. In matters other than military, the

writer whose reputation overtops all others is M. Frédéric
Masson.   His celebrity is such that it would be almost
impertinence to cavil at his writings.   For painstaking
and careful accumulation of evidence he stands far and
away above all his contemporaries.   He examines and
brings to notice every single detail.   A catalogue of an
Empress's chemises interests him as deeply as a list of a
Council of State.   The trouble is that his catalogue of
chemises is merely a catalogue of chemises—as interesting
as a laundress's bill.   M. Masson's books are exceedingly
important and invaluable to the student: but that they
are important and invaluable is all one can say about
them.

The ultimate source of much information is, of course,
the endless collection of volumes of Napoleon's correspondence.   Even merely to glance at one of these is a
lesson in industry far more thorough than anything
achieved by the worthy Dr. Samuel Smiles and his like.
Examination of a single day's correspondence is sufficient
to show the complexity of Napoleon's interests, the extent
of his knowledge of each subject, and the nature of the
driving power which built up the First Empire.   Close
study of the Correspondence is necessary to enable one
to follow the twists and turns of Napoleon's policy; the
main difficulty is that the bundle of hay is so large that
the finding of needles in it is a painfully tedious business.
However, the casual reader will find that this spadework
has been done for him by a large number of painstaking
writers.   Even during the present century several English
authors have published books upon particular events and
persons of the Napoleonic era.   Mr. Hilliard Atteridge is
an example of those who have done the best work in this
direction.   But the greater number of these books seem
to be struck with the same blight—they are ineffably
tedious.   Generally they are most correct as to facts;
their impartiality is admirable; the knowledge displayed
is wide; but they are most terribly boring to read.   They

are useful to familiarize the reader with the various persons described so that their place in the whole period is better understood, for the Napoleonic era is a tangled skein of threads, each of them a different personality, wound round and completely dependent upon the central core, which is Napoleon.

Of biographies and general histories it is impossible to speak definitely. Napoleon can boast hundreds more lives than any cat in fact or fancy. The percentage of lies contained in books on Napoleon varies between ten and ninety—and what is more aggravating is that the picturesque and readable lives are usually those which contain the most inexactitudes. It is perfectly safe to say that no Life of Napoleon has ever been written which combines complete accuracy with genuine readableness. This is of small account, however, for one has only to read enough of the readable and inexact lives to form a fairly correct opinion on most matters of importance at the same time as one enjoys both the reading and the forming of the opinion. The contemporary memoirs are very useful, and are mainly interesting. Bourrienne's biography is rather overrated usually, for he is unreliable in personal matters, and a great deal of his book is undeniably heavy. One of his most illuminating pictures shows Napoleon driving with him over the countryside, and ignoring the beauty of the scenery in favour of the military features of the landscape. This anecdote receives an additional interest when it is recalled that an exactly similar story is told of von Schlieffen, the German Chief of Staff of the 'nineties, who planned the advance through Belgium which had such vast consequences in 1914. One certainly cannot help thinking that if Napoleon had been at the head of the German army at that date he, too, would have advanced through Belgium, and this tiny parallel offers curious corroboration. Such a move would have been in complete accordance with Napoleon's character—compare Bernadotte's march through Anspach in 1805. The way in which Napoleon took enormous risks, such as this, and his method of securing the friendship of other Powers by storming and bluster instead of by finesse, is the most curious trait of his whole curious character. Bourrienne offers several examples; so do Talleyrand, Fouché, Pasquier and Molé.

For some decades after Napoleon's death an immense amount of spurious or heavily revised reminiscent literature appeared. Constant (the valet), Josephine, and various others, are credited with volumes of ingeniously written memoirs. They are well worth reading, but they contain little worth remembering. In many matters they are demonstrably incorrect, and they are generally prejudiced and misleading. For personal and intimate details one of the best contemporary writers is de Bausset, who certainly wrote the book which bears his name, and who equally certainly was in a position to perceive what he described, for he was a palace official for many years under the Empire.

In military matters the Marshals' memoirs are peculiarly enlightening, not so much in matters of detail (in fact they are frequently incorrect there) but in exhibiting the characters of the writers themselves. Davout's book is just what one would expect of him, cold and unrelenting and yet sound and brilliant. Suchet's is cynical and clever and subtle, and, if necessary, untrue. St. Cyr's displays his jealousy, suspicion and general unpleasantness along with undoubted proof of talent. Macdonald's is bluff and honest. There is a whole host of smaller fry, from Marbot downwards, who wrote fascinating little books about the Army and their own personal experiences. Some of them, such as the Reminiscences of Colonel de Gonneville, have appeared in English. They are all obtainable in French. The last authority, of course, on military matters is the Correspondence. There are only one or two doubtful letters in the whole collection, and these are either printed with reserve or bear the proofs of their spuriousness on the face of them.

But no matter how much is written, or published, or read, no two men will ever form quite the same estimate of Napoleon. It is as easy to argue that he only rose through sheer good luck as it is to argue that he only fell through sheer bad luck. He can be compared to Iscariot or to St. Paul, to Alexander or to Wilhelm II. At times he seems a body without a soul; at others, a soul without a body. All this seems to indicate that he was a man of contradictions, but on the other hand he was, admittedly, thoroughly consistent in all his actions. The most one can hope for is to form one's own conclusions about him; one cannot hope to form other people's.

INDEX

.

PRINTED IN GREAT BRITAIN BY THE NORTHUMBERLAND PRESS LIMITED
WATERLOO HOUSE, THORNTON STREET, NEWCASTLE-UPON-TYNE